ALOLA REGION HANDBOOK

Scholastic Inc.

All rights reserved. Published by Scholastic Inc., *Publishers since 1920*. SCHOLASTIC and associated logos are trademarks and/or registered trademarks of Scholastic Inc.

The publisher does not have any control over and does not assume any responsibility for author or third-party websites or their content.

No part of this publication may be reproduced, stored in a retrieval system, or transmitted in any form or by any means, electronic, mechanical, photocopying, recording, or otherwise, without written permission of the publisher. For information regarding permission, write to Scholastic Inc., Attention: Permissions Department, 557 Broadway, New York, NY 10012.

This book is a work of fiction. Names, characters, places, and incidents are either the product of the author's imagination or are used fictitiously, and any resemblance to actual persons, living or dead, business establishments, events, or locales is entirely coincidental.

ISBN 978-1-338-14862-6

10 9 8 7 6 5 4 3 2   17 18 19 20 21

Printed in the U.S.A.   40
First printing 2017
Designed by Two Red Shoes Design and Becky James

CONTENTS

WELCOME TO ALOLA!

There's so much to explore in this sunny new region—and dozens of exciting new Pokémon to discover.

The key to success with Pokémon is staying informed. Information about each Pokémon's type, category, height, and weight can make all the difference in catching, raising, battling, and evolving your Pokémon.

In this book, you'll get the stats and facts you need about the Pokémon of Alola. You'll find out how each Pokémon evolves and which moves it uses.

YOUR MISSION

COLLECT AND TRAIN AS MANY POKÉMON AS YOU CAN!

You'll start your journey by choosing one of three Pokémon . . .

POPPLIO

ROWLET

LITTEN

Once you have your first Pokémon, you can catch other Pokémon—and battle other Pokémon!

SO GET READY, TRAINERS: Soon you'll be ready to master almost any Pokémon challenge! To keep learning, just turn the page . . .

POKÉMON ARE CREATURES THAT COME IN ALL SHAPES, SIZES, AND PERSONALITIES.

Some live in oceans; others in caves, old towers, rivers, or tall grass. Trainers can find, capture, train, trade, collect, and use Pokémon in battle against their rivals in the quest to become top Pokémon Trainers.

This book contains over 250 known species of Pokémon. For most species, there are many individual Pokémon. Some are very common, like Rattata. You can find them almost anywhere. Others—like Lunala, Solgaleo, and Magearna—are classified as Legendary or Mythical Pokémon. They are extremely rare.

Each individual Pokémon has its own personality. For example, there are a lot of Pikachu, but Ash has a very special one who travels with him on all his adventures.

A Trainer's goal is to catch and befriend Pokémon in the wild and then train them to battle one another. Pokémon do not get seriously hurt in battle. If they are defeated, they faint and then return to their Poké Balls to rest and be healed. A Trainer's job is to take good care of his or her Pokémon.

HOW TO USE THIS BOOK

This book will provide the basic stats and facts you need to know to start your Pokémon journey. Here's what you'll discover about each Pokémon:

NAME

SPECIES

All Pokémon belong to a certain species.

HOW TO SAY IT

When it comes to Pokémon pronunciation, it's easy to get tongue-tied! There are many Pokémon with unusual names, so we'll help you sound them out. Soon you'll be saying Pokémon names so perfectly, you'll sound like a professor!

TYPE

Each Pokémon has a type, and some even have two! (Pokémon with two types are called dual-type Pokémon.) Every Pokémon type comes with advantages and disadvantages. We'll break them all down for you here.

HEIGHT AND WEIGHT

How does each Pokémon measure up? Find out by checking its height and weight stats. And remember, good things come in all shapes and sizes. It's up to every Trainer to work with his or her Pokémon and play up its strengths.

POSSIBLE MOVES

Every Pokémon has its own unique combination of moves. Before you hit the battlefield, we'll tell you all about each Pokémon's awesome attacks. And don't forget—with a good Trainer, they can always learn more!

DESCRIPTION

Knowledge is power! Pokémon Trainers have to know their stuff. Find out everything you need to know about your Pokémon here.

EVOLUTION

If your Pokémon has an evolved form or pre-evolved form, we'll show you its place in the chain and how it evolves.

LITTEN

Fire Cat Pokémon

- **How to Say It:** LIT-n
- **Type:** Fire
- **Imperial Height:** 1'04"
- **Metric Height:** 0.4 m
- **Imperial Weight:** 9.5 lbs.
- **Metric Weight:** 4.3 kg
- **Possible Moves:** Scratch, Ember, Growl, Lick, Leer, Fire Fang, Roar, Bite, Swagger, Fury Swipes, Thrash, Flamethrower, Scary Face, Flare Blitz, Outrage
- When it grooms its fur, Litten is storing up ammunition—the flaming fur is later coughed up in a fiery attack. Trainers often have a hard time getting this solitary Pokémon to trust them.

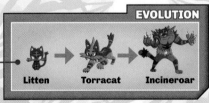

EVOLUTION

Litten → Torracat → Incineroar

88

Curious about what Pokémon types you'll spot on your journey? Find out more about types on the next page . . .

GUIDE TO POKÉMON TYPES

TYPE IS THE KEY TO UNLOCKING A POKÉMON'S POWER.

A Pokémon's type can tell you a lot about it—from where to find it in the wild to the moves it'll be able to use on the battlefield. For example, Water-type Pokémon usually live in lakes, oceans, and rivers, and use moves like Bubble and Hydro Pump.

A clever Trainer should always consider type when picking a Pokémon for a match, because type shows a Pokémon's strengths and weaknesses. For example, a Fire-type may melt an Ice-type, but against a Water-type, it might find it's the one in hot water. And while a Water-type usually has the upper hand in battle with a Fire-type, a Water-type move would act like a sprinkler on a Grass-type Pokémon. But when that same Grass-type is battling a Fire-type, it just might get scorched.

THE POKÉMON IN THIS BOOK HAVE EIGHTEEN DIFFERENT TYPES...

BUG

DARK

DRAGON

ELECTRIC

FAIRY

FIGHTING

FIRE

FLYING

GHOST

GRASS

GROUND

ICE

NORMAL

POISON

PSYCHIC

ROCK

STEEL

WATER

BATTLE BASICS

WHY BATTLE?

There are two basic reasons for a Pokémon to battle. One is for sport. You can battle another Trainer in a friendly competition. Your Pokémon do the fighting, but you decide which Pokémon and which moves to use.

The second reason is to catch wild Pokémon. Wild Pokémon have no training and no owners. They can be found pretty much anywhere. Battle is one of the main ways to catch a Pokémon. But other Trainers' Pokémon are off-limits. You can't capture their Pokémon, even if you win a competition.

AERODACTYL

Fossil Pokémon

How to Say It: AIR-row-DACK-tull

Type: Rock-Flying

Imperial Height: 5'11"

Metric Height: 1.8 m

Imperial Weight: 130.1 lbs.

Metric Weight: 59.0 kg

Possible Moves: Ice Fang, Fire Fang, Thunder Fang, Wing Attack, Supersonic, Bite, Scary Face, Roar, Agility, Ancient Power, Crunch, Take Down, Sky Drop, Iron Head, Hyper Beam, Rock Slide, Giga Impact

In its own time, this ancient Pokémon was master of the skies. The fangs that line its jaws are like the teeth of a saw, and it uses them to grip and tear at opponents.

EVOLUTION
Does not evolve.

ALAKAZAM

Psi Pokémon

How to Say It: AL-a-kuh-ZAM

Type: Psychic

Imperial Height: 4'11"

Metric Height: 1.5 m

Imperial Weight: 105.8 lbs.

Metric Weight: 48.0 kg

Possible Moves: Kinesis, Teleport, Confusion, Disable, Psybeam, Miracle Eye, Reflect, Psycho Cut, Recover, Telekinesis, Ally Switch, Psychic, Calm Mind, Future Sight, Trick

Alakazam's brain never stops growing, and its head has to keep expanding to contain its enormous intellect. If its psychic powers overflow, everyone nearby will get a splitting headache.

EVOLUTION

Abra → Kadabra → Alakazam

ALOMOMOLA

Caring Pokémon

How to Say It: uh-LOH-muh-MOH-luh
Type: Water
Imperial Height: 3'11"
Metric Height: 1.2 m
Imperial Weight: 69.7 lbs.
Metric Weight: 31.6 kg
Possible Moves: Play Nice, Pound, Water Sport, Aqua Ring, Aqua Jet, Double Slap, Heal Pulse, Protect, Water Pulse, Wake-Up Slap, Soak, Wish, Brine, Safeguard, Whirlpool, Helping Hand, Healing Wish, Wide Guard, Hydro Pump

Alomomola has a reputation as a healer in the open sea where it lives. Pokémon that have been hurt gather around it so it can fix them up with the curative slime that covers its body.

EVOLUTION
Does not evolve.

ARAQUANID

Water Bubble Pokémon

How to Say It: uh-RACK-wuh-nid
Type: Water-Bug
Imperial Height: 5'11"
Metric Height: 1.8 m
Imperial Weight: 180.8 lbs.
Metric Weight: 82.0 kg
Possible Moves: Wide Guard, Soak, Bubble, Infestation, Spider Web, Bug Bite, Bubble Beam, Bite, Aqua Ring, Leech Life, Crunch, Lunge, Mirror Coat, Liquidation, Entrainment

In battle, Araquanid uses the water bubble that surrounds its head as a weapon, headbutting its opponents or cutting off their air. When it's not battling, it uses the bubble as a shield to protect its weaker companions.

EVOLUTION

Dewpider → Araquanid

ARCANINE

Legendary Pokémon

How to Say It: ARE-ka-nine

Type: Fire

Imperial Height: 6'03"

Metric Height: 1.9 m

Imperial Weight: 341.7 lbs.

Metric Weight: 155.0 kg

Possible Moves: Thunder Fang, Bite, Roar, Odor Sleuth, Fire Fang, Extreme Speed

Beautiful and majestic, Arcanine uses the flame that burns within it as fuel to run amazing distances. Ancient Eastern folklore speaks of this powerful Pokémon.

EVOLUTION

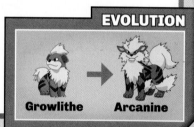

Growlithe → Arcanine

ARCHEN

First Bird Pokémon

How to Say It: AR-ken

Type: Rock-Flying

Imperial Height: 1'08"

Metric Height: 0.5 m

Imperial Weight: 20.9 lbs.

Metric Weight: 9.5 kg

Possible Moves: Quick Attack, Leer, Wing Attack, Rock Throw, Double Team, Scary Face, Pluck, Ancient Power, Agility, Quick Guard, Acrobatics, Dragon Breath, Crunch, Endeavor, U-turn, Rock Slide, Dragon Claw, Thrash

Although modern-day flying Pokémon are descended from Archen, this ancient Pokémon could not truly fly. It used its wings to glide between trees or swoop onto opponents from above.

EVOLUTION

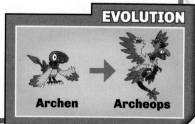

Archen → Archeops

ARCHEOPS

First Bird Pokémon

How to Say It: AR-kee-ops

Type: Rock-Flying

Imperial Height: 4'07"

Metric Height: 1.4 m

Imperial Weight: 70.5 lbs.

Metric Weight: 32.0 kg

Possible Moves: Quick Attack, Leer, Wing Attack, Rock Throw, Double Team, Scary Face, Pluck, Ancient Power, Agility, Quick Guard, Acrobatics, Dragon Breath, Crunch, Endeavor, U-turn, Rock Slide, Dragon Claw, Thrash

In the ancient world, Archeops could apparently fly but preferred to run, covering the ground at speeds of around 25 mph. They often teamed up against opponents—one would corner and distract the foe while another swooped in from above.

EVOLUTION

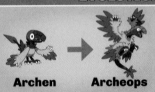

Archen → Archeops

ARIADOS

Long Leg Pokémon

How to Say It: AIR-ree-uh-dose

Type: Bug-Poison

Imperial Height: 3'07"

Metric Height: 1.1 m

Imperial Weight: 73.9 lbs.

Metric Weight: 33.5 kg

Possible Moves: Swords Dance, Focus Energy, Venom Drench, Fell Stinger, Bug Bite, Poison Sting, String Shot, Constrict, Absorb, Infestation, Scary Face, Night Shade, Shadow Sneak, Fury Swipes, Sucker Punch, Spider Web, Agility, Pin Missile, Psychic, Poison Jab, Cross Poison, Sticky Web, Toxic Thread

Ariados thread is sometimes used in weaving to produce a particularly strong piece of cloth. When making its web, Ariados spins this thread from both ends of its body.

EVOLUTION

Spinarak → Ariados

BAGON

Rock Head Pokémon

How to Say It: BAY-gon

Type: Dragon

Imperial Height: 2'00"

Metric Height: 0.6 m

Imperial Weight: 92.8 lbs.

Metric Weight: 42.1 kg

Possible Moves: Rage, Ember, Leer, Bite, Dragon Breath, Headbutt, Focus Energy, Crunch, Dragon Claw, Zen Headbutt, Scary Face, Flamethrower, Double-Edge

Frustrated by its lack of wings, Bagon goes around smashing things with its rocky head. Its single-minded pursuit of flight appears to be genetically motivated.

EVOLUTION

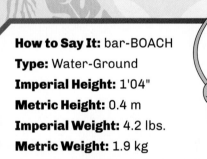

Bagon → Shelgon → Salamence

BARBOACH

Whiskers Pokémon

How to Say It: bar-BOACH

Type: Water-Ground

Imperial Height: 1'04"

Metric Height: 0.4 m

Imperial Weight: 4.2 lbs.

Metric Weight: 1.9 kg

Possible Moves: Mud-Slap, Mud Sport, Water Sport, Water Gun, Mud Bomb, Amnesia, Water Pulse, Magnitude, Rest, Snore, Aqua Tail, Earthquake, Muddy Water, Future Sight, Fissure

It's so hard to hold on to a slippery Barboach that doing so has become a competition in some places! This Pokémon prefers to live in muddy water, where it uses its whiskers to sense its surroundings.

EVOLUTION

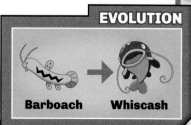

Barboach → Whiscash

BASTIODON

Shield Pokémon

How to Say It: BAS-tee-oh-DON

Type: Rock-Steel

Imperial Height: 4'03"

Metric Height: 1.3 m

Imperial Weight: 329.6 lbs.

Metric Weight: 149.5 kg

Possible Moves: Block, Tackle, Protect, Taunt, Metal Sound, Take Down, Iron Defense, Swagger, Ancient Power, Endure, Metal Burst, Iron Head, Heavy Slam

Bastiodon is well guarded against a frontal assault, but it's vulnerable from the rear. Fossils of Bastiodon and Rampardos have been discovered in the same places, often locked together in eternal combat.

EVOLUTION

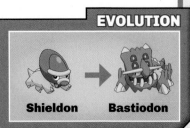

Shieldon → Bastiodon

BELDUM

Iron Ball Pokémon

How to Say It: BELL-dum

Type: Steel-Psychic

Imperial Height: 2'00"

Metric Height: 0.6 m

Imperial Weight: 209.9 lbs.

Metric Weight: 95.2 kg

Possible Move: Take Down

Groups of Beldum communicate using the power of magnetism. It uses the magnetic force generated inside its cells to pull its opponent within range of its claws.

EVOLUTION

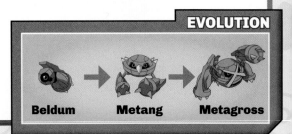

Beldum → Metang → Metagross

BEWEAR

Strong Arm Pokémon

How to Say It: beh-WARE

Type: Normal-Fighting

Imperial Height: 6'11"

Metric Height: 2.1 m

Imperial Weight: 297.6 lbs.

Metric Weight: 135.0 kg

Possible Moves: Tackle, Leer, Bide, Baby-Doll Eyes, Brutal Swing, Flail, Payback, Take Down, Hammer Arm, Thrash, Pain Split, Double-Edge, Superpower

Think twice before making friends with a Bewear. This superstrong Pokémon might be even more dangerous to those it likes, because it tends to deliver bone-crushing hugs as a sign of affection. Beware!

EVOLUTION

Stuffful → Bewear

21

BLISSEY

Happiness Pokémon

How to Say It: BLISS-sey

Type: Normal

Imperial Height: 4'11"

Metric Height: 1.5 m

Imperial Weight: 103.2 lbs.

Metric Weight: 46.8 kg

Possible Moves: Defense Curl, Pound, Growl, Tail Whip, Refresh, Double Slap, Soft-Boiled, Bestow, Minimize, Take Down, Sing, Fling, Heal Pulse, Egg Bomb, Light Screen, Healing Wish, Double-Edge

Eating the egg of a Blissey has a calming effect on even the wildest of tempers. The soft, fluffy fur that covers its body is extremely sensitive to its surroundings, and it can even sense emotions this way.

EVOLUTION

Happiny → Chansey → Blissey

BOLDORE

Ore Pokémon

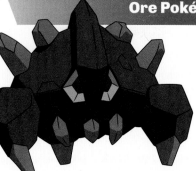

How to Say It: BOHL-dohr

Type: Rock

Imperial Height: 2'11"

Metric Height: 0.9 m

Imperial Weight: 224.9 lbs.

Metric Weight: 102.0 kg

Possible Moves: Power Gem, Tackle, Harden, Sand Attack, Headbutt, Rock Blast, Mud-Slap, Iron Defense, Smack Down, Rock Slide, Stealth Rock, Sandstorm, Stone Edge, Explosion

The crystals that dot Boldore's body are masses of pure energy and could be used as an impressive fuel source if they were to come off. It's good at finding underground water, but being near water makes it uneasy.

EVOLUTION

Roggenrola → Boldore → Gigalith

BONSLY

Bonsai Pokémon

How to Say It: BON-slye

Type: Rock

Imperial Height: 1'08"

Metric Height: 0.5 m

Imperial Weight: 33.1 lbs.

Metric Weight: 15.0 kg

Possible Moves: Fake Tears, Copycat, Flail, Low Kick, Rock Throw, Mimic, Feint Attack, Tearful Look, Rock Tomb, Block, Rock Slide, Counter, Sucker Punch, Double-Edge

Bonsly "sweats" by releasing moisture from its eyes, which makes it look like it's crying. It prefers a dry environment where few plants grow, but that often leaves it without camouflage.

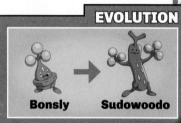

EVOLUTION

Bonsly → Sudowoodo

BOUNSWEET

Fruit Pokémon

How to Say It: BOWN*-sweet (*Rhymes with DOWN)

Type: Grass

Imperial Height: 1'00"

Metric Height: 0.3 m

Imperial Weight: 7.1 lbs.

Metric Weight: 3.2 kg

Possible Moves: Splash, Play Nice, Rapid Spin, Razor Leaf, Sweet Scent, Magical Leaf, Teeter Dance, Flail, Aromatic Mist

Bounsweet smells good enough to eat—which sometimes gets it into trouble! The intensely sugary liquid it gives off can be diluted to bring the sweetness level down so people can drink it.

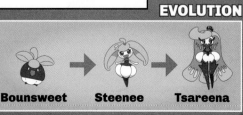

EVOLUTION

Bounsweet → Steenee → Tsareena

BRAVIARY

Valiant Pokémon

How to Say It: BRAY-vee-air-ee

Type: Normal-Flying

Imperial Height: 4'11"

Metric Height: 1.5 m

Imperial Weight: 90.4 lbs.

Metric Weight: 41.0 kg

Possible Moves: Thrash, Brave Bird, Whirlwind, Superpower, Peck, Leer, Fury Attack, Wing Attack, Hone Claws, Scary Face, Aerial Ace, Slash, Defog, Tailwind, Air Slash, Crush Claw, Sky Drop

In ancient Alola, Braviary was respected as "the hero of the sky." Several of these Pokémon teamed up to fight back against people who threatened their territory, or so the story goes.

EVOLUTION

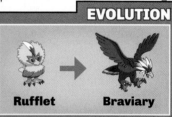

Rufflet → Braviary

BRIONNE

Pop Star Pokémon

How to Say It: bree-AHN

Type: Water

Imperial Height: 2'00"

Metric Height: 0.6 m

Imperial Weight: 38.6 lbs.

Metric Weight: 17.5 kg

Possible Moves: Pound, Water Gun, Growl, Disarming Voice, Baby-Doll Eyes, Aqua Jet, Encore, Bubble Beam, Sing, Double Slap, Hyper Voice, Moonblast, Captivate, Hydro Pump, Misty Terrain

Brionne pelts its opponents with water balloons in a swift and skillful battle dance. It also shows off its dancing abilities when trying to cheer up its Trainer.

EVOLUTION

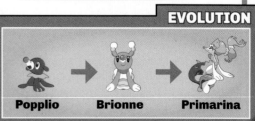

Popplio → Brionne → Primarina

BRUXISH

Gnash Teeth Pokémon

How to Say It: BRUCK-sish

Type: Water-Psychic

Imperial Height: 2'11"

Metric Height: 0.9 m

Imperial Weight: 41.9 lbs.

Metric Weight: 19.0 kg

Possible Moves: Water Gun, Astonish, Confusion, Bite, Aqua Jet, Disable, Psywave, Crunch, Aqua Tail, Screech, Psychic Fangs, Synchronoise

Don't let the beguiling grin of the brightly colored Bruxish fool you—those teeth are strong and sharp, and it can wield psychic powers mighty enough to stun an opponent in battle.

EVOLUTION
Does not evolve.

BUTTERFREE

Butterfly Pokémon

How to Say It: BUT-er-free

Type: Bug-Flying

Imperial Height: 3'07"

Metric Height: 1.1 m

Imperial Weight: 70.5 lbs.

Metric Weight: 32.0 kg

Possible Moves: Gust, Confusion, Poison Powder, Stun Spore, Sleep Powder, Psybeam, Silver Wind, Supersonic, Safeguard, Whirlwind, Bug Buzz, Rage Powder, Captivate, Tailwind, Air Slash, Quiver Dance

Butterfree's wings are covered in scales that carry poison. When attacked, it flutters its wings madly to scatter these scales. Its large compound eyes are formed of many tiny eyes.

EVOLUTION

Caterpie → Metapod → Butterfree

BUZZWOLE

Swollen Pokémon

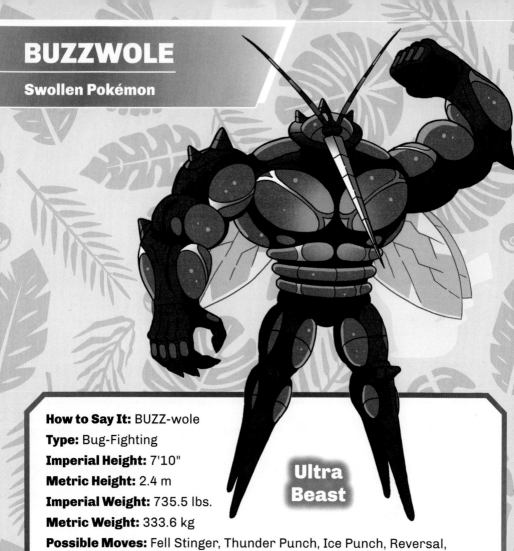

Ultra Beast

How to Say It: BUZZ-wole

Type: Bug-Fighting

Imperial Height: 7'10"

Metric Height: 2.4 m

Imperial Weight: 735.5 lbs.

Metric Weight: 333.6 kg

Possible Moves: Fell Stinger, Thunder Punch, Ice Punch, Reversal, Harden, Power-Up Punch, Focus Energy, Comet Punch, Bulk Up, Vital Throw, Endure, Leech Life, Taunt, Mega Punch, Counter, Hammer Arm, Lunge, Dynamic Punch, Superpower, Focus Punch

Buzzwole, one of the mysterious Ultra Beasts, is enormously strong, capable of demolishing heavy machinery with a punch. When it displays its impressive muscles, no one is sure whether it's just showing off—or issuing a threat.

EVOLUTION
Does not evolve.

CARBINK

Jewel Pokémon

EVOLUTION
Does not evolve.

How to Say It: CAR-bink

Type: Rock-Fairy

Imperial Height: 1'00"

Metric Height: 0.3 m

Imperial Weight: 12.6 lbs.

Metric Weight: 5.7 kg

Possible Moves: Tackle, Harden, Rock Throw, Sharpen, Smack Down, Reflect, Stealth Rock, Guard Split, Ancient Power, Flail, Skill Swap, Power Gem, Stone Edge, Moonblast, Light Screen, Safeguard

The extreme pressure and temperature of its underground home caused Carbink's body to compact and crystallize. Though it's not a rare Pokémon, the sparkle of its jewel-like body catches the eye.

CARRACOSTA

Prototurtle Pokémon

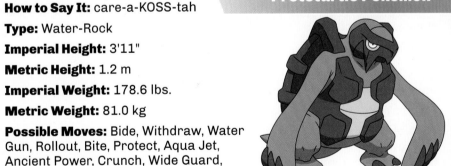

How to Say It: care-a-KOSS-tah

Type: Water-Rock

Imperial Height: 3'11"

Metric Height: 1.2 m

Imperial Weight: 178.6 lbs.

Metric Weight: 81.0 kg

Possible Moves: Bide, Withdraw, Water Gun, Rollout, Bite, Protect, Aqua Jet, Ancient Power, Crunch, Wide Guard, Brine, Smack Down, Curse, Shell Smash, Aqua Tail, Rock Slide, Rain Dance, Hydro Pump

Carracosta can get around pretty well on land and is a strong swimmer, which gives it an advantage in battles near water. Its heavy shell is made up of the same sturdy material as its bones.

EVOLUTION

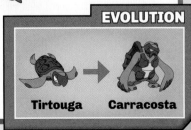

Tirtouga → Carracosta

CARVANHA

Savage Pokémon

How to Say It: car-VAH-na

Type: Water-Dark

Imperial Height: 2'07"

Metric Height: 0.8 m

Imperial Weight: 45.9 lbs.

Metric Weight: 20.8 kg

Possible Moves: Leer, Bite, Rage, Focus Energy, Aqua Jet, Assurance, Screech, Swagger, Ice Fang, Scary Face, Poison Fang, Crunch, Agility, Take Down

A lone Carvanha is a bit of a wimp, but in numbers they're terrifying. Any hint of blood in the water draws them swarming to attack. Each school defends its territory viciously.

EVOLUTION

Carvanha → Sharpedo

CASTFORM

Weather Pokémon

How to Say It: CAST-form

Type: Normal

Imperial Height: 1'00"

Metric Height: 0.3 m

Imperial Weight: 1.8 lbs.

Metric Weight: 0.8 kg

Possible Moves: Tackle, Water Gun, Ember, Powder Snow, Headbutt, Rain Dance, Sunny Day, Hail, Weather Ball, Hydro Pump, Fire Blast, Blizzard, Hurricane

When the weather changes, Castform's appearance changes with it. It's so sensitive to shifts in humidity and temperature that these changes alter the structure of its cells.

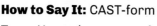

Snowy Form

Regular Form

Rainy Form

Sunny Form

EVOLUTION
Does not evolve.

CATERPIE

Worm Pokémon

How to Say It: CAT-ur-pee

Type: Bug

Imperial Height: 1'00"

Metric Height: 0.3 m

Imperial Weight: 6.4 lbs.

Metric Weight: 2.9 kg

Possible Moves: Tackle, String Shot, Bug Bite

Caterpie is recommended for Trainers just starting their journey—it doesn't require much effort to catch and raise this Pokémon. To repel the Flying-types that like to attack it, Caterpie produces a terrible smell from its antennae.

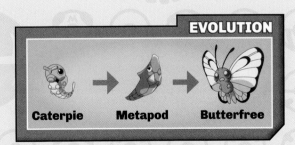

EVOLUTION

Caterpie → Metapod → Butterfree

CELESTEELA

Launch Pokémon

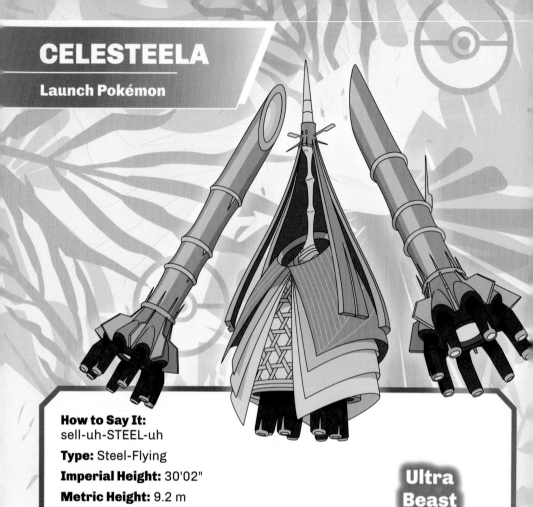

How to Say It:
sell-uh-STEEL-uh

Type: Steel-Flying

Imperial Height: 30'02"

Metric Height: 9.2 m

Imperial Weight: 2,204.4 lbs.

Metric Weight: 999.9 kg

Ultra Beast

Possible Moves: Wide Guard, Air Slash, Ingrain, Absorb, Harden, Tackle, Smack Down, Mega Drain, Leech Seed, Metal Sound, Iron Head, Giga Drain, Flash Cannon, Autotomize, Seed Bomb, Skull Bash, Iron Defense, Heavy Slam, Double-Edge

Celesteela, one of the mysterious Ultra Beasts, can shoot incendiary gases from its arms and has been known to burn down wide swaths of trees. In flight, it can reach impressive speeds.

EVOLUTION
Does not evolve.

CHANSEY

Egg Pokémon

How to Say It: CHAN-see

Type: Normal

Imperial Height: 3'07"

Metric Height: 1.1 m

Imperial Weight: 76.3 lbs.

Metric Weight: 34.6 kg

Possible Moves: Double-Edge, Defense Curl, Pound, Growl, Tail Whip, Refresh, Double Slap, Soft-Boiled, Bestow, Minimize, Take Down, Sing, Fling, Heal Pulse, Egg Bomb, Light Screen, Healing Wish

Many other Pokémon just love Chansey eggs—they're full of nutrients and very tasty. Chansey move fast and can be hard to find, so catching one is a rare treat.

EVOLUTION

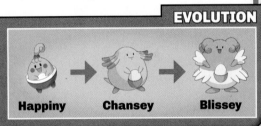

Happiny → Chansey → Blissey

CHARJABUG

Battery Pokémon

How to Say It: CHAR-juh-bug

Type: Bug-Electric

Imperial Height: 1'08"

Metric Height: 0.5 m

Imperial Weight: 23.1 lbs.

Metric Weight: 10.5 kg

Possible Moves: Charge, Vice Grip, String Shot, Mud-Slap, Bite, Bug Bite, Spark, Acrobatics, Crunch, X-Scissor, Dig, Discharge, Iron Defense

When Charjabug breaks down food for energy, some of that energy is stored as electricity inside its body. A Trainer who likes to go camping would appreciate having this Pokémon as a partner!

EVOLUTION

Grubbin → Charjabug → Vikavolt

CHINCHOU

Angler Pokémon

How to Say It: CHIN-chow

Type: Water-Electric

Imperial Height: 1'08"

Metric Height: 0.5 m

Imperial Weight: 26.5 lbs.

Metric Weight: 12.0 kg

Possible Moves: Bubble, Supersonic, Thunder Wave, Electro Ball, Water Gun, Confuse Ray, Bubble Beam, Spark, Signal Beam, Flail, Discharge, Take Down, Aqua Ring, Hydro Pump, Ion Deluge, Charge

Long ago, two of Chinchou's fins developed into antennae, which flash brightly to communicate with others, or to light its way in the depths of the ocean where it lives. They can also discharge an electric shock.

EVOLUTION

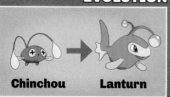

Chinchou → Lanturn

CLEFABLE

Fairy Pokémon

How to Say It: kleh-FAY-bull

Type: Fairy

Imperial Height: 4'03"

Metric Height: 1.3 m

Imperial Weight: 88.2 lbs.

Metric Weight: 40.0 kg

Possible Moves: Spotlight, Disarming Voice, Sing, Double Slap, Minimize, Metronome

Clefable usually stay hidden, living in the mountains far from people. Tradition holds that anyone who sees two Clefable skipping along together will have a happy marriage.

EVOLUTION

Cleffa → Clefairy → Clefable

CLEFAIRY

Fairy Pokémon

How to Say It: kleh-FAIR-ee

Type: Fairy

Imperial Height: 2'00"

Metric Height: 0.6 m

Imperial Weight: 16.5 lbs.

Metric Weight: 7.5 kg

Possible Moves: Spotlight, Disarming Voice, Pound, Growl, Encore, Sing, Double Slap, Defense Curl, Follow Me, Bestow, Wake-Up Slap, Minimize, Stored Power, Metronome, Cosmic Power, Lucky Chant, Body Slam, Moonlight, Moonblast, Gravity, Meteor Mash, Healing Wish, After You

Who doesn't love Clefairy? People of all ages think they're really adorable, but they can be hard to find. When they dance under the full moon, a strange magnetic force surrounds the area.

EVOLUTION

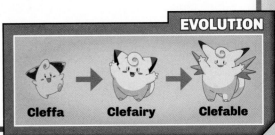

Cleffa   Clefairy   Clefable

CLEFFA

Star Shape Pokémon

How to Say It: CLEFF-uh

Type: Fairy

Imperial Height: 1'00"

Metric Height: 0.3 m

Imperial Weight: 6.6 lbs.

Metric Weight: 3.0 kg

Possible Moves: Pound, Charm, Encore, Sing, Sweet Kiss, Copycat, Magical Leaf

Cleffa who live in the Alola region are very fond of Minior. When shooting stars streak through the night sky, Cleffa can be found watching intently. With its five-pointed silhouette, it's said to be the rebirth of a star.

EVOLUTION

Cleffa   Clefairy   Clefable

CLOYSTER

Bivalve Pokémon

How to Say It: CLOY-stur

Type: Water-Ice

Imperial Height: 4'11"

Metric Height: 1.5 m

Imperial Weight: 292.1 lbs.

Metric Weight: 132.5 kg

Possible Moves: Hydro Pump, Shell Smash, Toxic Spikes, Withdraw, Supersonic, Protect, Aurora Beam, Spike Cannon, Spikes, Icicle Crash

Ancient people used the spikes from Cloyster shells to make spears. The shell is strong enough to withstand a bomb blast, so what lurks within remains a mystery.

EVOLUTION

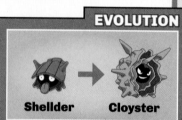

Shellder → Cloyster

COMFEY

Posy Picker Pokémon

How to Say It: KUM-fay

Type: Fairy

Imperial Height: 0'04"

Metric Height: 0.1 m

Imperial Weight: 0.7 lbs.

Metric Weight: 0.3 kg

Possible Moves: Helping Hand, Vine Whip, Flower Shield, Leech Seed, Draining Kiss, Magical Leaf, Growth, Wrap, Sweet Kiss, Natural Gift, Petal Blizzard, Synthesis, Sweet Scent, Grass Knot, Floral Healing, Petal Dance, Aromatherapy, Grassy Terrain, Play Rough

Comfey collects flowers and attaches them to its vine, where they flourish and release a calming fragrance. Adding these flowers to bathwater makes for a relaxing soak.

EVOLUTION
Does not evolve.

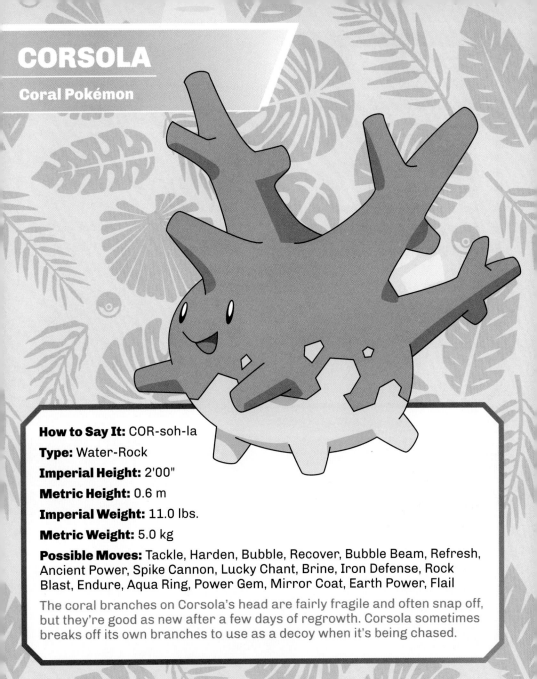

CORSOLA

Coral Pokémon

How to Say It: COR-soh-la

Type: Water-Rock

Imperial Height: 2'00"

Metric Height: 0.6 m

Imperial Weight: 11.0 lbs.

Metric Weight: 5.0 kg

Possible Moves: Tackle, Harden, Bubble, Recover, Bubble Beam, Refresh, Ancient Power, Spike Cannon, Lucky Chant, Brine, Iron Defense, Rock Blast, Endure, Aqua Ring, Power Gem, Mirror Coat, Earth Power, Flail

The coral branches on Corsola's head are fairly fragile and often snap off, but they're good as new after a few days of regrowth. Corsola sometimes breaks off its own branches to use as a decoy when it's being chased.

EVOLUTION
Does not evolve.

COSMOEM

Protostar Pokémon

How to Say It: KOZ-mo-em

Type: Psychic

Imperial Height: 0'04"

Metric Height: 0.1 m

Imperial Weight: 2,204.4 lbs.

Metric Weight: 999.9 kg

Possible Moves: Cosmic Power, Teleport

Cosmoem never moves, radiating a gentle warmth as it develops inside the hard shell that surrounds it. Long ago, people referred to it as the cocoon of the stars, and some still think its origins lie in another world.

EVOLUTION

Cosmog → Cosmoem → Solgaleo / Lunala

COSMOG

Nebula Pokémon

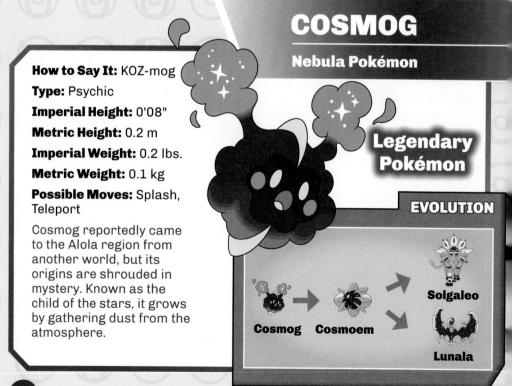

How to Say It: KOZ-mog

Type: Psychic

Imperial Height: 0'08"

Metric Height: 0.2 m

Imperial Weight: 0.2 lbs.

Metric Weight: 0.1 kg

Possible Moves: Splash, Teleport

Cosmog reportedly came to the Alola region from another world, but its origins are shrouded in mystery. Known as the child of the stars, it grows by gathering dust from the atmosphere.

EVOLUTION

Cosmog → Cosmoem → Solgaleo / Lunala

COTTONEE

Cotton Puff Pokémon

How to Say It: KAHT-ton-ee

Type: Grass-Fairy

Imperial Height: 1'00"

Metric Height: 0.3 m

Imperial Weight: 1.3 lbs.

Metric Weight: 0.6 kg

Possible Moves: Absorb, Fairy Wind, Growth, Leech Seed, Stun Spore, Mega Drain, Cotton Spore, Razor Leaf, Poison Powder, Giga Drain, Charm, Helping Hand, Energy Ball, Cotton Guard, Sunny Day, Endeavor, Solar Beam

When several Cottonee gather, they tend to huddle up and cling together in a big puffy cloud of soft, fluffy Pokémon. Such gatherings often leave behind drifts of cottony material that makes excellent stuffing for pillows and mattresses.

EVOLUTION

Cottonee → **Whimsicott**

CRABOMINABLE

Woolly Crab Pokémon

How to Say It: crab-BAH-min-uh-bull

Type: Fighting-Ice

Imperial Height: 5'07"

Metric Height: 1.7 m

Imperial Weight: 396.8 lbs.

Metric Weight: 180.0 kg

Possible Moves: Ice Punch, Bubble, Rock Smash, Leer, Pursuit, Bubble Beam, Power-Up Punch, Dizzy Punch, Avalanche, Reversal, Ice Hammer, Iron Defense, Dynamic Punch, Close Combat

Covered in warm fur, Crabominable evolved from Crabrawler that took their goal of aiming for the top a bit too literally and found themselves at the summit of icy mountains. They can detach their pincers and shoot them at foes.

EVOLUTION

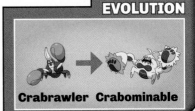

Crabrawler → **Crabominable**

37

CRABRAWLER

Boxing Pokémon

How to Say It: crab-BRAW-ler

Type: Fighting

Imperial Height: 2'00"

Metric Height: 0.6 m

Imperial Weight: 15.4 lbs.

Metric Weight: 7.0 kg

Possible Moves: Bubble, Rock Smash, Leer, Pursuit, Bubble Beam, Power-Up Punch, Dizzy Punch, Payback, Reversal, Crabhammer, Iron Defense, Dynamic Punch, Close Combat

Crabrawler is always looking for a fight, and it really hates to lose. Sometimes its pincers come right off because it uses them for punching so much! Fortunately, it can regrow them quickly.

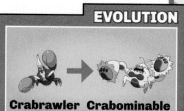

EVOLUTION

Crabrawler Crabominable

CRANIDOS

Head Butt Pokémon

How to Say It: CRANE-ee-dose

Type: Rock

Imperial Height: 2'11"

Metric Height: 0.9 m

Imperial Weight: 69.4 lbs.

Metric Weight: 31.5 kg

Possible Moves: Headbutt, Leer, Focus Energy, Pursuit, Take Down, Scary Face, Assurance, Chip Away, Ancient Power, Zen Headbutt, Screech, Head Smash

Fossilized trees, broken in half, are often found in the same area as Cranidos fossils. This Pokémon lived in the ancient jungle and also used its powerful headbutt to battle its rival, Aerodactyl.

EVOLUTION

Cranidos Rampardos

CROBAT

Bat Pokémon

How to Say It: CROW-bat

Type: Poison-Flying

Imperial Height: 5'11"

Metric Height: 1.8 m

Imperial Weight: 165.3 lbs.

Metric Weight: 75.0 kg

Possible Moves: Cross Poison, Screech, Absorb, Supersonic, Astonish, Bite, Wing Attack, Confuse Ray, Air Cutter, Swift, Poison Fang, Mean Look, Leech Life, Haze, Venoshock, Air Slash, Quick Guard

Crobat's hind legs evolved into an extra pair of wings, so this Pokémon has a hard time getting around on the ground. In the air, though, it's a master of speed and stealth.

EVOLUTION

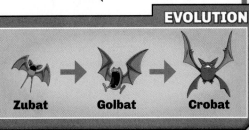

Zubat → Golbat → Crobat

CUBONE

Lonely Pokémon

How to Say It: CUE-bone

Type: Ground

Imperial Height: 1'04"

Metric Height: 0.4 m

Imperial Weight: 14.3 lbs.

Metric Weight: 6.5 kg

Possible Moves: Growl, Tail Whip, Bone Club, Headbutt, Leer, Focus Energy, Bonemerang, Rage, False Swipe, Thrash, Fling, Stomping Tantrum, Endeavor, Double-Edge, Retaliate, Bone Rush

When Cubone mourns for its lost mother, its loud cries sometimes attract the attention of Mandibuzz, who swoop down to attack. Some think that learning to cope with its grief is the only way Cubone can evolve.

EVOLUTION

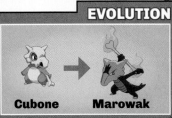

Cubone → Marowak

CUTIEFLY

Bee Fly Pokémon

How to Say It: KYOO-tee-fly

Type: Bug-Fairy

Imperial Height: 0'04"

Metric Height: 0.1 m

Imperial Weight: 0.4 lbs

Metric Weight: 0.2 kg

Possible Moves: Absorb, Fairy Wind, Stun Spore, Struggle Bug, Silver Wind, Draining Kiss, Sweet Scent, Bug Buzz, Dazzling Gleam, Aromatherapy, Quiver Dance

Cutiefly can sense the aura of flowers and gauge when they're ready to bloom, so it always knows where to find fresh nectar. If you notice a swarm of these Pokémon following you around, you might have a floral aura!

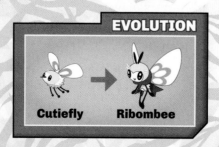

EVOLUTION

Cutiefly → Ribombee

DARTRIX

Blade Quill Pokémon

How to Say It: DAR-trix

Type: Grass-Flying

Imperial Height: 2'04"

Metric Height: 0.7 m

Imperial Weight: 35.3 lbs.

Metric Weight: 16.0 kg

Possible Moves: Tackle, Leafage, Growl, Peck, Astonish, Razor Leaf, Foresight, Pluck, Synthesis, Fury Attack, Sucker Punch, Leaf Blade, Feather Dance, Brave Bird, Nasty Plot

Dartrix is very conscious of its appearance and spends a lot of time keeping its wings clean. It can throw sharp-edged feathers, known as blade quills, with great accuracy.

EVOLUTION

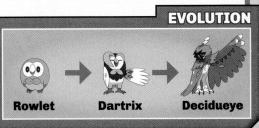

Rowlet → Dartrix → Decidueye

DECIDUEYE

Arrow Quill Pokémon

How to Say It: deh-SIH-joo-eye

Type: Grass-Ghost

Imperial Height: 5'03"

Metric Height: 1.6 m

Imperial Weight: 80.7 lbs.

Metric Weight: 36.6 kg

Possible Moves: Spirit Shackle, U-turn, Tackle, Leafage, Growl, Peck, Astonish, Razor Leaf, Foresight, Pluck, Synthesis, Fury Attack, Sucker Punch, Leaf Blade, Feather Dance, Brave Bird, Nasty Plot

A natural marksman, Decidueye can shoot its arrow quills with astonishing precision, hitting a tiny target a hundred yards away. It tends to be calm and collected, but sometimes panics if it's caught off guard.

EVOLUTION

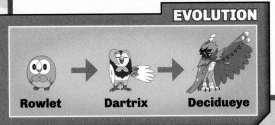

Rowlet → Dartrix → Decidueye

DELIBIRD

Delivery Pokémon

How to Say It: DELL-ee-bird

Type: Ice-Flying

Imperial Height: 2'11"

Metric Height: 0.9 m

Imperial Weight: 35.3 lbs.

Metric Weight: 16.0 kg

Possible Moves: Present, Drill Peck

Delibird usually live in very cold climates, but they seem to be fairly tolerant of the tropical heat of Alola. Most of their time is spent trying to build up food supplies that they then share with others.

EVOLUTION
Does not evolve.

DEWPIDER

Water Bubble Pokémon

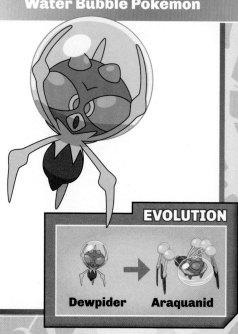

How to Say It: DOO-pih-der

Type: Water-Bug

Imperial Height: 1'00"

Metric Height: 0.3 m

Imperial Weight: 8.8 lbs.

Metric Weight: 4.0 kg

Possible Moves: Water Sport, Bubble, Infestation, Spider Web, Bug Bite, Bubble Beam, Bite, Aqua Ring, Leech Life, Crunch, Lunge, Mirror Coat, Liquidation, Entrainment

Mostly aquatic, Dewpider brings a water-bubble "helmet" along when it ventures onto the land to look for food. The bubble also lends extra power when it headbutts an opponent.

EVOLUTION

Dewpider → Araquanid

DHELMISE

Sea Creeper Pokémon

How to Say It: dell-MIZE

Type: Ghost-Grass

Imperial Height: 12'10"

Metric Height: 3.9 m

Imperial Weight: 463.0 lbs.

Metric Weight: 210.0 kg

Possible Moves: Switcheroo, Absorb, Growth, Rapid Spin, Astonish, Mega Drain, Wrap, Gyro Ball, Metal Sound, Giga Drain, Whirlpool, Anchor Shot, Shadow Ball, Energy Ball, Slam, Heavy Slam, Phantom Force, Power Whip

When Dhelmise swings its mighty anchor, even the biggest Pokémon have to watch out! It snags seaweed floating past on the waves and scavenges detritus from the seafloor to add to its body.

EVOLUTION
Does not evolve.

DIGLETT (Alola Form)

Mole Pokémon

How to Say It: DIG-let

Type: Ground-Steel

Imperial Height: 0'08"

Metric Height: 0.2 m

Imperial Weight: 2.2 lbs.

Metric Weight: 1.0 kg

Possible Moves: Sand Attack, Metal Claw, Growl, Astonish, Mud-Slap, Magnitude, Bulldoze, Sucker Punch, Mud Bomb, Earth Power, Dig, Iron Head, Earthquake, Fissure

The metal hairs that sprout from the top of Diglett's head can be used to communicate or to sense its surroundings. It can extend just those hairs aboveground to make sure everything is safe before emerging.

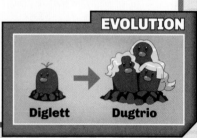

EVOLUTION

Diglett → Dugtrio

DITTO

Transform Pokémon

How to Say It: DIT-toe

Type: Normal

Imperial Height: 1'00"

Metric Height: 0.3 m

Imperial Weight: 8.8 lbs.

Metric Weight: 4.0 kg

Possible Move: Transform

Ditto can change its shape to resemble just about anything, and it sometimes uses this talent to befriend other Pokémon. Some are more skilled at duplication than others.

EVOLUTION
Does not evolve.

DRAGONAIR

Dragon Pokémon

How to Say It: DRAG-gon-AIR

Type: Dragon

Imperial Height: 13'01"

Metric Height: 4.0 m

Imperial Weight: 36.4 lbs.

Metric Weight: 16.5 kg

Possible Moves: Wrap, Leer, Thunder Wave, Twister, Dragon Rage, Slam, Agility, Dragon Tail, Aqua Tail, Dragon Rush, Safeguard, Dragon Dance, Outrage, Hyper Beam

With the crystalline orbs on its body, Dragonair is rumored to be able to change the weather. Because of this, farmers have long regarded this Pokémon with respect.

EVOLUTION

Dratini → Dragonair → Dragonite

DRAGONITE

Dragon Pokémon

How to Say It: DRAG-gon-ite

Type: Dragon-Flying

Imperial Height: 7'03"

Metric Height: 2.2 m

Imperial Weight: 463.0 lbs.

Metric Weight: 210.0 kg

Possible Moves: Wing Attack, Hurricane, Fire Punch, Thunder Punch, Roost, Wrap, Leer, Thunder Wave, Twister, Dragon Rage, Slam, Agility, Dragon Tail, Aqua Tail, Dragon Rush, Safeguard, Dragon Dance, Outrage, Hyper Beam, Hurricane

A Dragonite once rescued a man from a shipwreck and flew him off to a Dragonite paradise on a faraway island. This calm and kindly Pokémon is slow to anger, but once roused, its wrath can be incredibly destructive.

EVOLUTION

Dratini → Dragonair → Dragonite

DRAMPA

Placid Pokémon

How to Say It: DRAM-puh

Type: Normal-Dragon

Imperial Height: 9'10"

Metric Height: 3.0 m

Imperial Weight: 407.9 lbs.

Metric Weight: 185.0 kg

Possible Moves: Play Nice, Echoed Voice, Twister, Protect, Glare, Light Screen, Dragon Rage, Natural Gift, Dragon Breath, Safeguard, Extrasensory, Dragon Pulse, Fly, Hyper Voice, Outrage

Even wild Drampa have a real soft spot for kids. Though they make their home far away in the mountains, they often come into town to visit and play with the local children.

EVOLUTION
Does not evolve.

DRATINI

Dragon Pokémon

How to Say It: dra-TEE-nee

Type: Dragon

Imperial Height: 5'11"

Metric Height: 1.8 m

Imperial Weight: 7.3 lbs.

Metric Weight: 3.3 kg

Possible Moves: Wrap, Leer, Thunder Wave, Twister, Dragon Rage, Slam, Agility, Dragon Tail, Aqua Tail, Dragon Rush, Safeguard, Dragon Dance, Outrage, Hyper Beam

Dratini's existence was mere rumor until a fisherman finally managed to catch one after fighting it for many long hours. It sheds its skin several times as it grows, and the skin is sometimes used in clothing.

EVOLUTION

Dratini   Dragonair   Dragonite

DRIFBLIM

Blimp Pokémon

How to Say It: DRIFF-blim

Type: Ghost-Flying

Imperial Height: 3'11"

Metric Height: 1.2 m

Imperial Weight: 33.1 lbs.

Metric Weight: 15.0 kg

Possible Moves: Phantom Force, Constrict, Minimize, Astonish, Gust, Focus Energy, Payback, Ominous Wind, Stockpile, Hex, Swallow, Spit Up, Shadow Ball, Amnesia, Baton Pass, Explosion

Drifblim take to the sky at dusk, flying in large groups. They can be hard to track even for a dedicated observer because they sometimes disappear right in front of people's eyes.

EVOLUTION

Drifloon → **Drifblim**

DRIFLOON

Balloon Pokémon

How to Say It: DRIFF-loon

Type: Ghost-Flying

Imperial Height: 1'04"

Metric Height: 0.4 m

Imperial Weight: 2.6 lbs.

Metric Weight: 1.2 kg

Possible Moves: Constrict, Minimize, Astonish, Gust, Focus Energy, Payback, Ominous Wind, Stockpile, Hex, Swallow, Spit Up, Shadow Ball, Amnesia, Baton Pass, Explosion

Scary stories are told of children who took hold of Drifloon's dangling strings and were never seen again. The spirit within its floating body is only barely contained—any puncture could send it spilling out with a ghostly shriek.

EVOLUTION

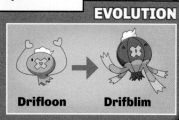

Driloon → **Drifblim**

DROWZEE

Hypnosis Pokémon

How to Say It: DROW-zee

Type: Psychic

Imperial Height: 3'03"

Metric Height: 1.0 m

Imperial Weight: 71.4 lbs

Metric Weight: 32.4 kg

Possible Moves: Pound, Hypnosis, Disable, Confusion, Poison Gas, Meditate, Psybeam, Headbutt, Psych Up, Synchronoise, Zen Headbutt, Swagger, Psychic, Nasty Plot, Psyshock, Future Sight

Drowzee feeds on dreams and has a particular taste for the ones that show the dreamer having a lot of fun. It sometimes shows off its favorite dreams to friends.

EVOLUTION

Drowzee → Hypno

DUGTRIO (Alola Form)

Mole Pokémon

How to Say It: DUG-TREE-oh

Type: Ground-Steel

Imperial Height: 2'04"

Metric Height: 0.7 m

Imperial Weight: 146.8 lbs.

Metric Weight: 66.6 kg

Possible Moves: Sand Tomb, Rototiller, Night Slash, Tri Attack, Sand Attack, Metal Claw, Growl, Astonish, Mud-Slap, Magnitude, Bulldoze, Sucker Punch, Mud Bomb, Earth Power, Dig, Iron Head, Earthquake, Fissure

Although Dugtrio's golden hair is shiny and beautiful, people aren't inclined to collect it when it falls—there are stories that doing so will bring bad luck. In Alola, this Pokémon is thought to represent the spirit of the land.

EVOLUTION

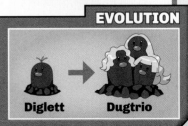

Diglett → Dugtrio

EEVEE
Evolution Pokémon

How to Say It: EE-vee

Type: Normal

Imperial Height: 1'00"

Metric Height: 0.3 m

Imperial Weight: 14.3 lbs.

Metric Weight: 6.5 kg

Possible Moves: Covet, Helping Hand, Growl, Tackle, Tail Whip, Sand Attack, Baby-Doll Eyes, Quick Attack, Bite, Swift, Refresh, Take Down, Charm, Baton Pass, Double-Edge, Last Resort, Trump Card

Eight different Pokémon evolve from the amazingly adaptive Eevee, according to current studies. Its unstable genetic structure allows for this incredible diversity in Evolution.

EVOLUTION

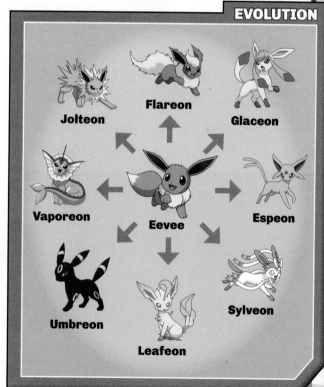

Jolteon

Flareon

Glaceon

Vaporeon

Eevee

Espeon

Umbreon

Leafeon

Sylveon

ELECTABUZZ

Electric Pokémon

How to Say It:
eh-LECK-ta-buzz

Type: Electric

Imperial Height: 3'07"

Metric Height: 1.1 m

Imperial Weight: 66.1 lbs.

Metric Weight: 30.0 kg

Possible Moves: Quick Attack, Leer, Thunder Shock, Low Kick, Swift, Shock Wave, Thunder Wave, Electro Ball, Light Screen, Thunder Punch, Discharge, Screech, Thunderbolt, Thunder

Electabuzz consumes electricity but isn't very good at retaining the power within its body—it's constantly leaking electric current. If the power goes out on a calm, sunny day, it's probably the fault of Electabuzz.

EVOLUTION

Elekid → Electabuzz → Electivire

ELECTIVIRE

Thunderbolt Pokémon

How to Say It:
el-LECT-uh-vire

Type: Electric

Imperial Height: 5'11"

Metric Height: 1.8 m

Imperial Weight: 305.6 lbs.

Metric Weight: 138.6 kg

Possible Moves: Electric Terrain, Ion Deluge, Fire Punch, Quick Attack, Leer, Thunder Shock, Low Kick, Swift, Shock Wave, Thunder Wave, Electro Ball, Light Screen, Thunder Punch, Discharge, Screech, Thunderbolt, Thunder, Giga Impact, Electric Terrain

When Electivire beats its chest in excitement, it produces a sound like thunder and showers of electric sparks. It can unleash an intense shock by pressing the tips of its two tails into its foe.

EVOLUTION

Elekid → Electabuzz → Electivire

ELEKID

Electric Pokémon

How to Say It: EL-eh-kid

Type: Electric

Imperial Height: 2'00"

Metric Height: 0.6 m

Imperial Weight: 51.8 lbs.

Metric Weight: 23.5 kg

Possible Moves: Quick Attack, Leer, Thunder Shock, Low Kick, Swift, Shock Wave, Thunder Wave, Electro Ball, Light Screen, Thunder Punch, Discharge, Screech, Thunderbolt, Thunder

An Elekid that lives with its Trainer can feed on electricity straight from the outlets in the house. These Pokémon have developed a rivalry with Togedemaru, who try to siphon off their electricity.

EVOLUTION

Elekid → Electabuzz → Electivire

EMOLGA

Sky Squirrel Pokémon

How to Say It: ee-MAHL-guh

Type: Electric-Flying

Imperial Height: 1'04"

Metric Height: 0.4 m

Imperial Weight: 11.0 lbs.

Metric Weight: 5.0 kg

Possible Moves: Thunder Shock, Quick Attack, Tail Whip, Charge, Spark, Nuzzle, Pursuit, Double Team, Shock Wave, Electro Ball, Acrobatics, Light Screen, Encore, Volt Switch, Agility, Discharge

When Emolga stretches out its limbs, the membrane connecting them spreads like a cape and allows it to glide through the air. The holes that Pikipek drill in trees make handy nests for wild Emolga.

EVOLUTION
Does not evolve.

ESPEON

Sun Pokémon

How to Say It: ESS-pee-on

Type: Psychic

Imperial Height: 2'11"

Metric Height: 0.9 m

Imperial Weight: 58.4 lbs.

Metric Weight: 26.5 kg

Possible Moves: Confusion, Helping Hand, Tackle, Tail Whip, Sand Attack, Baby-Doll Eyes, Quick Attack, Swift, Psybeam, Future Sight, Psych Up, Morning Sun, Psychic, Last Resort, Power Swap

Espeon doesn't have to see its opponent to sense its movements—its fine fur picks up even the slightest shift in air currents. If the orb on its forehead goes dark, that means its psychic power is temporarily depleted.

EVOLUTION

Eevee → Espeon

EXEGGCUTE

Egg Pokémon

How to Say It: ECKS-egg-cute

Type: Grass-Psychic

Imperial Height: 1'04"

Metric Height: 0.4 m

Imperial Weight: 5.5 lbs.

Metric Weight: 2.5 kg

Possible Moves: Barrage, Uproar, Hypnosis, Reflect, Leech Seed, Bullet Seed, Stun Spore, Poison Powder, Sleep Powder, Confusion, Worry Seed, Natural Gift, Solar Beam, Extrasensory, Bestow

Exeggcute is made up of six eggs that communicate with one another using telepathy. Crabrawler sometimes seeks out this Pokémon to pick a fight, but it can't stand up to Exeggcute's psychic powers.

EVOLUTION

Exeggcute → Exeggutor

EXEGGUTOR (Alola Form)

Coconut Pokémon

How to Say It: ecks-EGG-u-tore

Type: Grass-Dragon

Imperial Height: 35'09"

Metric Height: 10.9 m

Imperial Weight: 916.2 lbs.

Metric Weight: 415.6 kg

Possible Moves: Dragon Hammer, Seed Bomb, Barrage, Hypnosis, Confusion, Psyshock, Egg Bomb, Wood Hammer, Leaf Storm

In the tropical sun and sand, Exeggutor grows exceptionally tall, unlocking draconic powers hidden deep within. Trainers in Alola are proud of the tree-like Exeggutor and consider this to be its ideal form.

EVOLUTION

Exeggcute → Exeggutor

53

FEAROW

Beak Pokémon

How to Say It: FEER-oh

Type: Normal-Flying

Imperial Height: 3'11"

Metric Height: 1.2 m

Imperial Weight: 83.8 lbs.

Metric Weight: 38.0 kg

Possible Moves: Drill Run, Pluck, Peck, Growl, Leer, Pursuit, Fury Attack, Aerial Ace, Mirror Move, Assurance, Agility, Focus Energy, Roost, Drill Peck

It's unclear how long Fearow has been around, but ancient artwork seems to depict this long-beaked Pokémon. Its untiring wings enable it to fly the whole day through, even when it's carrying something heavy.

EVOLUTION

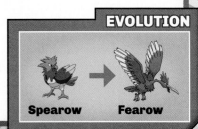

Spearow → Fearow

FEEBAS

Fish Pokémon

How to Say It: FEE-bass

Type: Water

Imperial Height: 2'00"

Metric Height: 0.6 m

Imperial Weight: 16.3 lbs.

Metric Weight: 7.4 kg

Possible Moves: Splash, Tackle, Flail

The rather shabby Feebas won't win any beauty contests, but it's a hardy Pokémon that can live happily even in dirty water. Researchers are trying to figure out what makes it so tough.

EVOLUTION

Feebas → Milotic

FINNEON

Wing Fish Pokémon

How to Say It: FINN-ee-on

Type: Water

Imperial Height: 1'04"

Metric Height: 0.4 m

Imperial Weight: 15.4 lbs.

Metric Weight: 7.0 kg

Possible Moves: Pound, Water Gun, Attract, Rain Dance, Gust, Water Pulse, Captivate, Safeguard, Aqua Ring, Whirlpool, U-turn, Bounce, Silver Wind, Soak

With its twin tails, Finneon can leap high out of the water to absorb sunlight, making the pink markings on its body shine. Sometimes a nearby Wingull notices and swoops down to attack.

EVOLUTION

Finneon → Lumineon

FLAREON

Flame Pokémon

How to Say It: FLAIR-ee-on

Type: Fire

Imperial Height: 2'11"

Metric Height: 0.9 m

Imperial Weight: 55.1 lbs.

Metric Weight: 25.0 kg

Possible Moves: Ember, Helping Hand, Tackle, Tail Whip, Sand Attack, Baby-Doll Eyes, Quick Attack, Bite, Fire Fang, Fire Spin, Scary Face, Smog, Lava Plume, Last Resort, Flare Blitz

Flareon prefers to roast berries with its fiery breath before chowing down. The temperature of its body averages nearly 1,500 degrees Fahrenheit—and the sac where it stores its flames is twice as hot!

EVOLUTION

Eevee → Flareon

FLETCHINDER

Ember Pokémon

How to Say It:
FLETCH-in-der

Type: Fire-Flying

Imperial Height: 2'04"

Metric Height: 0.7 m

Imperial Weight: 35.3 lbs.

Metric Weight: 16.0 kg

Possible Moves: Ember, Tackle, Growl, Quick Attack, Peck, Agility, Flail, Roost, Razor Wind, Natural Gift, Flame Charge, Acrobatics, Me First, Tailwind, Steel Wing

Each Fletchinder jealously guards its own territory and drives intruders away. Flaming embers shoot forth from its beak to attack—or to grill its food to perfection before eating.

EVOLUTION

Fletchling   Fletchinder   Talonflame

FLETCHLING

Tiny Robin Pokémon

How to Say It: FLETCH-ling

Type: Normal-Flying

Imperial Height: 1'00"

Metric Height: 0.3 m

Imperial Weight: 3.7 lbs.

Metric Weight: 1.7 kg

Possible Moves: Tackle, Growl, Quick Attack, Peck, Agility, Flail, Roost, Razor Wind, Natural Gift, Flame Charge, Acrobatics, Me First, Tailwind, Steel Wing

Fletchling is generally calm and friendly, an easy partner for a beginning Trainer—but when called upon, it battles with a fierce determination. In the excitement, its body temperature spikes sharply.

EVOLUTION

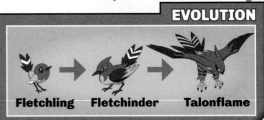

Fletchling   Fletchinder   Talonflame

FLYGON

Mystic Pokémon

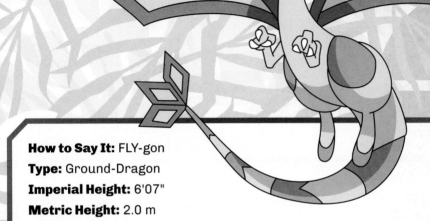

How to Say It: FLY-gon

Type: Ground-Dragon

Imperial Height: 6'07"

Metric Height: 2.0 m

Imperial Weight: 180.8 lbs.

Metric Weight: 82.0 kg

Possible Moves: Dragon Claw, Dragon Breath, Dragon Dance, Sand Attack, Sonic Boom, Feint Attack, Bide, Mud-Slap, Bulldoze, Sand Tomb, Rock Slide, Supersonic, Screech, Earth Power, Dragon Tail, Earthquake, Sandstorm, Uproar, Hyper Beam, Dragon Rush

Flygon is rarely seen, but can sometimes be heard in the desert—when it flaps its wings, the vibrations give off a sound like singing. It stirs up sandstorms to hide itself and confuse opponents.

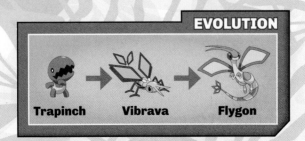

EVOLUTION

Trapinch → Vibrava → Flygon

FOMANTIS

Sickle Grass Pokémon

How to Say It: fo-MAN-tis

Type: Grass

Imperial Height: 1'00"

Metric Height: 0.3 m

Imperial Weight: 3.3 lbs.

Metric Weight: 1.5 kg

Possible Moves: Fury Cutter, Leafage, Razor Leaf, Growth, Ingrain, Leaf Blade, Synthesis, Slash, Sweet Scent, Solar Beam, Sunny Day

Fomantis sleeps the day away, basking in the sunlight. The sweet scent it gives off sometimes attracts Cutiefly to its hiding place. During the night, it seeks out a safe place to sleep for the next day.

EVOLUTION

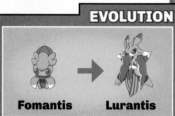

Fomantis   **Lurantis**

FROSLASS

Snow Land Pokémon

How to Say It: FROS-lass

Type: Ice-Ghost

Imperial Height: 4'03"

Metric Height: 1.3 m

Imperial Weight: 58.6 lbs.

Metric Weight: 26.6 kg

Possible Moves: Ominous Wind, Destiny Bond, Powder Snow, Leer, Double Team, Ice Shard, Icy Wind, Astonish, Draining Kiss, Will-O-Wisp, Confuse Ray, Wake-Up Slap, Captivate, Shadow Ball, Blizzard, Hail

Apparently, the first Froslass came into being when a woman was lost while exploring the snowy mountains. The frozen statues that decorate its icy lair may not be statues . . .

EVOLUTION

Snorunt   **Froslass**

GABITE

Cave Pokémon

How to Say It: gab-BITE

Type: Dragon-Ground

Imperial Height: 4'07"

Metric Height: 1.4 m

Imperial Weight: 123.5 lbs.

Metric Weight: 56.0 kg

Possible Moves: Dual Chop, Tackle, Sand Attack, Dragon Rage, Sandstorm, Take Down, Sand Tomb, Slash, Dragon Claw, Dig, Dragon Rush

Gabite doesn't shed often, so its cast-off scales are hard to find, but they're a valuable ingredient in medicine. It hoards shiny things—including Carbink—in the cave where it lives.

EVOLUTION

Gible → Gabite → Garchomp

GARBODOR

Trash Heap Pokémon

How to Say It: gar-BOH-dur

Type: Poison

Imperial Height: 6'03"

Metric Height: 1.9 m

Imperial Weight: 236.6 lbs.

Metric Weight: 107.3 kg

Possible Moves: Pound, Poison Gas, Recycle, Toxic Spikes, Acid Spray, Double Slap, Sludge, Stockpile, Swallow, Body Slam, Sludge Bomb, Clear Smog, Toxic, Amnesia, Belch, Gunk Shot, Explosion

Garbodor were once a common sight in Alola, but since Grimer were brought in to deal with a pollution problem, competition for the same food source has reduced their numbers. The liquid they shoot from their arms is toxic.

EVOLUTION

Trubbish → Garbodor

GARCHOMP

Mach Pokémon

How to Say It: GAR-chomp
Type: Dragon-Ground
Imperial Height: 6'03"
Metric Height: 1.9 m
Imperial Weight: 209.4 lbs.
Metric Weight: 95.0 kg
Possible Moves: Crunch, Dual Chop, Fire Fang, Tackle, Sand Attack, Dragon Rage, Sandstorm, Take Down, Sand Tomb, Slash, Dragon Claw, Dig, Dragon Rush

Garchomp could win a race against a jet plane as it zooms through the skies. Some flying Pokémon have learned that colliding with a Garchomp moving at top speed is extremely dangerous.

EVOLUTION

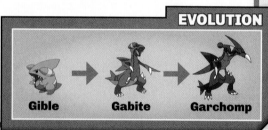

Gible → Gabite → Garchomp

GASTLY

Gas Pokémon

How to Say It: GAST-lee
Type: Ghost-Poison
Imperial Height: 4'03"
Metric Height: 1.3 m
Imperial Weight: 0.2 lbs.
Metric Weight: 0.1 kg
Possible Moves: Hypnosis, Lick, Spite, Mean Look, Curse, Night Shade, Confuse Ray, Sucker Punch, Payback, Shadow Ball, Dream Eater, Dark Pulse, Destiny Bond, Hex, Nightmare

Gastly likes to lurk in abandoned buildings, where its presence sometimes causes strange lights to flicker. This gaseous Pokémon is hard to see, but it gives off a surprisingly delicate, sweet scent.

EVOLUTION

Gastly → Haunter → Gengar

GASTRODON (EAST SEA)

Sea Slug Pokémon

How to Say It: GAS-stroh-don

Type: Water-Ground

Imperial Height: 2'11"

Metric Height: 0.9 m

Imperial Weight: 65.9 lbs.

Metric Weight: 29.9 kg

Possible Moves: Mud-Slap, Mud Sport, Harden, Water Pulse, Mud Bomb, Hidden Power, Rain Dance, Body Slam, Muddy Water, Recover

Color variations between Gastrodon from different habitats have intrigued scientists for some time. Research is under way to find out what happens when a blue East Sea Gastrodon is moved to western seas.

EVOLUTION

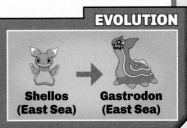

Shellos (East Sea) → Gastrodon (East Sea)

GASTRODON (WEST SEA)

Sea Slug Pokémon

How to Say It: GAS-stroh-don

Type: Water-Ground

Imperial Height: 2'11"

Metric Height: 0.9 m

Imperial Weight: 65.9 lbs.

Metric Weight: 29.9 kg

Possible Moves: Mud-Slap, Mud Sport, Harden, Water Pulse, Mud Bomb, Hidden Power, Rain Dance, Body Slam, Muddy Water, Recover

If West Sea Gastrodon loses a part of its squishy pink body, it can regenerate. It sometimes comes forth from the seas to wander on land, and no one really knows why.

EVOLUTION

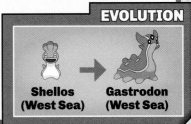

Shellos (West Sea) → Gastrodon (West Sea)

GENGAR

Shadow Pokémon

How to Say It: GHEN-gar

Type: Ghost-Poison

Imperial Height: 4'11"

Metric Height: 1.5 m

Imperial Weight: 89.3 lbs.

Metric Weight: 40.5 kg

Possible Moves: Shadow Punch, Hypnosis, Lick, Spite, Mean Look, Curse, Night Shade, Confuse Ray, Sucker Punch, Payback, Shadow Ball, Dream Eater, Dark Pulse, Destiny Bond, Hex, Nightmare

The sudden onset of an unexplained chill might mean a Gengar is coming toward you. This Pokémon seems to have misunderstood the concept of "making friends"—it tries to create a kindred spirit by attacking humans.

EVOLUTION

Gastly → Haunter → Gengar

GEODUDE (Alola Form)

Rock Pokémon

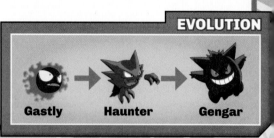

How to Say It: JEE-oh-dude

Type: Rock-Electric

Imperial Height: 1'04"

Metric Height: 0.4 m

Imperial Weight: 44.8 lbs.

Metric Weight: 20.3 kg

Possible Moves: Tackle, Defense Curl, Charge, Rock Polish, Rollout, Spark, Rock Throw, Smack Down, Thunder Punch, Self-Destruct, Stealth Rock, Rock Blast, Discharge, Explosion, Double-Edge, Stone Edge

In the Alola region, Geodude are naturally magnetic, and their bodies are often covered in iron particles they've picked up while sleeping in the sand. Stepping on one can cause a nasty shock, so beachgoers keep a sharp eye out.

EVOLUTION

Geodude → Graveler → Golem

GIBLE

Land Shark Pokémon

How to Say It: GIB-bull

Type: Dragon-Ground

Imperial Height: 2'04"

Metric Height: 0.7 m

Imperial Weight: 45.2 lbs.

Metric Weight: 20.5 kg

Possible Moves: Tackle, Sand Attack, Dragon Rage, Sandstorm, Take Down, Sand Tomb, Slash, Dragon Claw, Dig, Dragon Rush

Gible are drawn to cozy caves that are kept warm by geothermal energy. Even in their warm caves, they tend to huddle together when the outside weather gets too cold. A passerby might get an unexpected chomping!

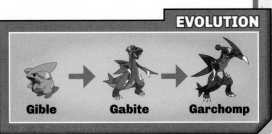

EVOLUTION

Gible → Gabite → Garchomp

GIGALITH

Compressed Pokémon

How to Say It: GIH-gah-lith

Type: Rock

Imperial Height: 5'07"

Metric Height: 1.7 m

Imperial Weight: 573.2 lbs.

Metric Weight: 260.0 kg

Possible Moves: Power Gem, Tackle, Harden, Sand Attack, Headbutt, Rock Blast, Mud-Slap, Iron Defense, Smack Down, Rock Slide, Stealth Rock, Sandstorm, Stone Edge, Explosion

On a clear day, Gigalith can absorb sunlight and convert the energy into amazingly powerful blasts. This doesn't work in the rain or after dark, though. It often helps out around construction sites.

EVOLUTION

Roggenrola → Boldore → Gigalith

GLACEON

Fresh Snow Pokémon

How to Say It: GLAY-cee-on

Type: Ice

Imperial Height: 2'07"

Metric Height: 0.8 m

Imperial Weight: 57.1 lbs.

Metric Weight: 25.9 kg

Possible Moves: Icy Wind, Helping Hand, Tackle, Tail Whip, Sand Attack, Baby-Doll Eyes, Quick Attack, Bite, Ice Fang, Ice Shard, Barrier, Mirror Coat, Hail, Last Resort, Blizzard

The icy Glaceon has amazing control over its body temperature. It can freeze its own fur and then smash into an opponent with the spiky icicles that result.

EVOLUTION

Eevee → Glaceon

GLALIE

Face Pokémon

How to Say It: GLAY-lee

Type: Ice

Imperial Height: 4'11"

Metric Height: 1.5 m

Imperial Weight: 565.5 lbs.

Metric Weight: 256.5 kg

Possible Moves: Freeze-Dry, Sheer Cold, Powder Snow, Leer, Double Team, Ice Shard, Icy Wind, Bite, Ice Fang, Headbutt, Protect, Frost Breath, Crunch, Blizzard, Hail

When Glalie breathes icy air from its gaping mouth, it can instantly freeze its opponent. It apparently came into being from a rock on a mountainside soaking up the despair of a climber lost in the cold.

EVOLUTION

Snorunt → Glalie

GOLBAT

Bat Pokémon

How to Say It: GOHL-bat

Type: Poison-Flying

Imperial Height: 5'03"

Metric Height: 1.6 m

Imperial Weight: 121.3 lbs.

Metric Weight: 55.0 kg

Possible Moves: Screech, Absorb, Supersonic, Astonish, Bite, Wing Attack, Confuse Ray, Air Cutter, Swift, Poison Fang, Mean Look, Leech Life, Haze, Venoshock, Air Slash, Quick Guard

Golbat's fangs are hollow, which allows it to suck up blood for its meals more efficiently. This efficiency can cause problems, though—sometimes it eats so much that it has trouble flying afterward!

EVOLUTION

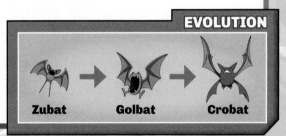

Zubat   Golbat   Crobat

GOLDEEN

Goldfish Pokémon

How to Say It: GOL-deen

Type: Water

Imperial Height: 2'00"

Metric Height: 0.6 m

Imperial Weight: 33.1 lbs.

Metric Weight: 15.0 kg

Possible Moves: Peck, Tail Whip, Water Sport, Supersonic, Horn Attack, Flail, Water Pulse, Aqua Ring, Fury Attack, Waterfall, Horn Drill, Agility, Soak, Megahorn

Seeing a school of Goldeen swimming upstream brings joy to anyone who's been pining for the return of spring. Some Trainers are such huge fans that they ignore other Pokémon and devote all their time only to Goldeen.

EVOLUTION

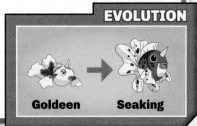

Goldeen   Seaking

GOLDUCK

Duck Pokémon

How to Say It: GOL-duck

Type: Water

Imperial Height: 5'07"

Metric Height: 1.7 m

Imperial Weight: 168.9 lbs.

Metric Weight: 76.6 kg

Possible Moves: Me First, Aqua Jet, Water Sport, Scratch, Tail Whip, Water Gun, Disable, Confusion, Fury Swipes, Water Pulse, Screech, Zen Headbutt, Aqua Tail, Soak, Psych Up, Amnesia, Hydro Pump, Wonder Room

People used to think they could gain mysterious powers by taking the red orb from Golduck's forehead. It keeps an eye out for underwater Pokémon as it patrols near the edge of its lake home.

EVOLUTION

Psyduck → Golduck

GOLEM (Alola Form)

Megaton Pokémon

How to Say It: GO-lum

Type: Rock-Electric

Imperial Height: 5'07"

Metric Height: 1.7 m

Imperial Weight: 696.7 lbs.

Metric Weight: 316.0 kg

Possible Moves: Heavy Slam, Tackle, Defense Curl, Charge, Rock Polish, Steamroller, Spark, Rock Throw, Smack Down, Thunder Punch, Self-Destruct, Stealth Rock, Rock Blast, Discharge, Explosion, Double-Edge, Stone Edge

The rocks Golem fires from its back carry a strong electrical charge, so even a glancing blow can deliver a powerful shock. Sometimes it grabs a Geodude to fire instead.

EVOLUTION

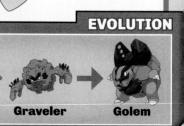

Geodude → Graveler → Golem

GOLISOPOD

Hard Scale Pokémon

How to Say It: go-LIE-suh-pod

Type: Bug-Water

Imperial Height: 6'07"

Metric Height: 2.0 m

Imperial Weight: 238.1 lbs.

Metric Weight: 108.0 kg

Possible Moves: First Impression, Struggle Bug, Sand Attack, Fury Cutter, Rock Smash, Bug Bite, Spite, Swords Dance, Slash, Razor Shell, Sucker Punch, Iron Defense, Pin Missile, Liquidation

When Golisopod has to battle, its six sharp-clawed arms are certainly up to the task. Most of the time, though, it lives quietly in underwater caves, where it meditates and avoids conflict.

EVOLUTION

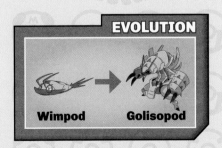

Wimpod → Golisopod

GOODRA

Dragon Pokémon

How to Say It:
GOO-druh

Type: Dragon

Imperial Height: 6'07"

Metric Height: 2.0 m

Imperial Weight: 331.8 lbs.

Metric Weight: 150.5 kg

Possible Moves: Aqua Tail, Outrage, Feint, Tackle, Bubble, Absorb, Protect, Bide, Dragon Breath, Rain Dance, Flail, Body Slam, Muddy Water, Dragon Pulse, Power Whip

Goodra loves to make friends and gets very sad when it's on its own for too long. When bullied, this apparently meek Pokémon goes into attack mode, swinging its hefty tail and horns.

EVOLUTION

Goomy → Sliggoo → Goodra

GOOMY

Soft Tissue Pokémon

How to Say It: GOO-mee

Type: Dragon

Imperial Height: 1'00"

Metric Height: 0.3 m

Imperial Weight: 6.2 lbs.

Metric Weight: 2.8 kg

Possible Moves: Tackle, Bubble, Absorb, Protect, Bide, Dragon Breath, Rain Dance, Flail, Body Slam, Muddy Water, Dragon Pulse

The slimy membrane that covers Goomy's body provides it with protection—partly by keeping others away because touching it is really gross! It stays in the shade to keep itself from drying out.

EVOLUTION

Goomy → Sliggoo → Goodra

GRANBULL

Fairy Pokémon

How to Say It:
GRAN-bull

Type: Fairy

Imperial Height: 4'07"

Metric Height: 1.4 m

Imperial Weight: 107.4 lbs.

Metric Weight: 48.7 kg

Possible Moves: Outrage, Ice Fang, Fire Fang, Thunder Fang, Tackle, Scary Face, Tail Whip, Charm, Bite, Lick, Headbutt, Roar, Rage, Play Rough, Payback, Crunch

With its massive fangs and strong jaw, Granbull looks like a fierce opponent—but it's a total sweetheart, a timid Pokémon who bites only when provoked. This amusing contrast has made it popular among young people.

EVOLUTION

Snubbull → **Granbull**

GRAVELER (Alola Form)

Rock Pokémon

How to Say It:
GRAV-el-ler

Type: Rock-Electric

Imperial Height: 3'03"

Metric Height: 1.0 m

Imperial Weight: 242.5 lbs.

Metric Weight: 110.0 kg

Possible Moves: Tackle, Defense Curl, Charge, Rock Polish, Rollout, Spark, Rock Throw, Smack Down, Thunder Punch, Self-Destruct, Stealth Rock, Rock Blast, Discharge, Explosion, Double-Edge, Stone Edge

The crystals that appear on Graveler's body are the result of consuming dravite, a particularly tasty mineral. Graveler often fight over dravite deposits, crashing together with a sound like thunder.

EVOLUTION

Geodude → **Graveler** → **Golem**

GRIMER (Alola Form)

Sludge Pokémon

How to Say It: GRY-mur

Type: Poison-Dark

Imperial Height: 2'04"

Metric Height: 0.7 m

Imperial Weight: 92.6 lbs.

Metric Weight: 42.0 kg

Possible Moves: Pound, Poison Gas, Harden, Bite, Disable, Acid Spray, Poison Fang, Minimize, Fling, Knock Off, Crunch, Screech, Gunk Shot, Acid Armor, Belch, Memento

Grimer's appearance in the Alola region developed after it was called upon to deal with a persistent garbage problem. Each crystal on its body is formed from dangerous toxins, and those toxins escape if a crystal falls off.

EVOLUTION

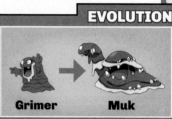

Grimer   Muk

GROWLITHE

Puppy Pokémon

How to Say It: GROWL-lith

Type: Fire

Imperial Height: 2'04"

Metric Height: 0.7 m

Imperial Weight: 41.9 lbs.

Metric Weight: 19.0 kg

Possible Moves: Bite, Roar, Ember, Leer, Odor Sleuth, Helping Hand, Flame Wheel, Reversal, Fire Fang, Take Down, Flame Burst, Agility, Retaliate, Flamethrower, Crunch, Heat Wave, Outrage, Flare Blitz

If you try to pet another Trainer's Growlithe, you'll soon discover this Pokémon isn't just cute—it has a fiercely territorial side. It's known for its intelligence and loyalty.

EVOLUTION

Growlithe   Arcanine

GRUBBIN

Larva Pokémon

How to Say It:
GRUB-bin

Type: Bug

Imperial Height: 1'04"

Metric Height: 0.4 m

Imperial Weight: 9.7 lbs.

Metric Weight: 4.4 kg

Possible Moves: Vice Grip, String Shot, Mud-Slap, Bite, Bug Bite, Spark, Acrobatics, Crunch, X-Scissor, Dig

Grubbin have discovered that sticking close to Electric-type Pokémon offers some protection from the Flying-types that often like to attack them! With their strong jaws, they can scrape away tree bark to get at the delicious sap underneath.

EVOLUTION

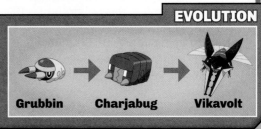

Grubbin → Charjabug → Vikavolt

GUMSHOOS

Stakeout Pokémon

How to Say It: GUM-shooss

Type: Normal

Imperial Height: 2'04"

Metric Height: 0.7 m

Imperial Weight: 31.3 lbs.

Metric Weight: 14.2 kg

Possible Moves: Tackle, Leer, Pursuit, Sand Attack, Odor Sleuth, Bide, Bite, Mud-Slap, Super Fang, Take Down, Scary Face, Crunch, Hyper Fang, Yawn, Thrash, Rest

Gumshoos displays amazing patience when it's on a stakeout, waiting to ambush its prey. It's a natural enemy of Rattata, but the two rarely interact because they're awake at different times.

EVOLUTION

Yungoos → Gumshoos

GUZZLORD

Junkivore Pokémon

How to Say It: GUZZ-lord

Type: Dark-Dragon

Imperial Height: 18'01"

Metric Height: 5.5 m

Imperial Weight: 1,957.7 lbs.

Metric Weight: 888.0 kg

Ultra Beast

Possible Moves: Belch, Wide Guard, Swallow, Stockpile, Dragon Rage, Bite, Stomp, Brutal Swing, Steamroller, Dragon Tail, Iron Tail, Stomping Tantrum, Crunch, Hammer Arm, Thrash, Gastro Acid, Heavy Slam, Wring Out, Dragon Rush

Guzzlord, one of the mysterious Ultra Beasts, seems to have an insatiable appetite for just about everything—it will even swallow buildings and mountains. This constant munching can be very destructive.

EVOLUTION
Does not evolve.

GYARADOS

Atrocious Pokémon

How to Say It: GARE-uh-dos

Type: Water-Flying

Imperial Height: 21'04"

Metric Height: 6.5 m

Imperial Weight: 518.1 lbs.

Metric Weight: 235.0 kg

Possible Moves: Bite, Thrash, Leer, Twister, Ice Fang, Aqua Tail, Scary Face, Dragon Rage, Crunch, Hydro Pump, Dragon Dance, Hurricane, Rain Dance, Hyper Beam

Gyarados is incredibly destructive, and its temper is legendary. Stories say it once burned an entire town to the ground in one night after the residents offended it in some way.

EVOLUTION

Magikarp → Gyarados

HAKAMO-O

Scaly Pokémon

How to Say It:
HAH-kah-MOH-oh

Type: Dragon-Fighting

Imperial Height: 3'11"

Metric Height: 1.2 m

Imperial Weight: 103.6 lbs.

Metric Weight: 47.0 kg

Possible Moves: Sky Uppercut, Autotomize, Tackle, Leer, Bide, Protect, Dragon Tail, Scary Face, Headbutt, Work Up, Screech, Iron Defense, Dragon Claw, Noble Roar, Dragon Dance, Outrage

Hakamo-o regularly sheds its scales and grows new ones. Each set of scales is harder and sharper than the one before. It leaps at opponents with a battle cry, and the sharp scales turn its punches into a real threat.

EVOLUTION

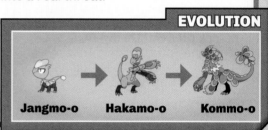

Jangmo-o → Hakamo-o → Kommo-o

HAPPINY

Playhouse Pokémon

How to Say It: hap-PEE-nee

Type: Normal

Imperial Height: 2'00"

Metric Height: 0.6 m

Imperial Weight: 53.8 lbs.

Metric Weight: 24.4 kg

Possible Moves: Pound, Charm, Copycat, Refresh, Sweet Kiss

In the pouch on its belly, Happiny carefully stores a round white stone that resembles an egg. It sometimes offers this stone to those it likes.

EVOLUTION

Happiny → Chansey → Blissey

73

HARIYAMA

Arm Thrust Pokémon

How to Say It:
HAR-ee-YAH-mah

Type: Fighting

Imperial Height: 7'07"

Metric Height: 2.3 m

Imperial Weight: 559.5 lbs.

Metric Weight: 253.8 kg

Possible Moves: Brine, Tackle, Focus Energy, Sand Attack, Arm Thrust, Fake Out, Force Palm, Whirlwind, Knock Off, Vital Throw, Belly Drum, Smelling Salts, Seismic Toss, Wake-Up Slap, Endure, Close Combat, Reversal, Heavy Slam

Hariyama is so strong that a single strike from its open palm can fling a truck into the air. Older Hariyama tend to channel that strength into training Makuhita instead of competing with each other.

EVOLUTION

Makuhita → Hariyama

HAUNTER

Gas Pokémon

How to Say It: HAUNT-ur

Type: Ghost-Poison

Imperial Height: 5'03"

Metric Height: 1.6 m

Imperial Weight: 0.2 lbs.

Metric Weight: 0.1 kg

Possible Moves: Hypnosis, Lick, Spite, Mean Look, Curse, Night Shade, Confuse Ray, Sucker Punch, Payback, Shadow Ball, Dream Eater, Dark Pulse, Destiny Bond, Hex, Nightmare

Getting licked by the cold tongue of a Haunter is more than simply unpleasant—such a lick can steal your life energy. These Pokémon live in darkness, and city lights can drive them away.

EVOLUTION

Gastly → Haunter → Gengar

HERDIER

Loyal Dog Pokémon

How to Say It: HERD-ee-er

Type: Normal

Imperial Height: 2'11"

Metric Height: 0.9 m

Imperial Weight: 32.4 lbs.

Metric Weight: 14.7 kg

Possible Moves: Leer, Tackle, Odor Sleuth, Bite, Helping Hand, Take Down, Work Up, Crunch, Roar, Retaliate, Reversal, Last Resort, Giga Impact, Play Rough

Herdier's black fur is so dense that it forms a hard, protective layer, and it grows all the time. Keeping the fur groomed can be a challenge, but many Trainers find it worthwhile because Herdier is such a loyal partner.

EVOLUTION

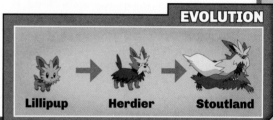

Lillipup → Herdier → Stoutland

HONCHKROW

Big Boss Pokémon

How to Say It: HONCH-krow

Type: Dark-Flying

Imperial Height: 2'11"

Metric Height: 0.9 m

Imperial Weight: 60.2 lbs.

Metric Weight: 27.3 kg

Possible Moves: Sucker Punch, Astonish, Pursuit, Haze, Wing Attack, Swagger, Nasty Plot, Foul Play, Night Slash, Quash, Dark Pulse

Honchkrow keeps an army of Murkrow at its beck and call, ruling by intimidation. The underlings know that if they don't keep Honchkrow fed, it won't hesitate to punish them.

EVOLUTION

Murkrow → Honchkrow

HYPNO

Hypnosis Pokémon

How to Say It: HIP-no

Type: Psychic

Imperial Height: 5'03"

Metric Height: 1.6 m

Imperial Weight: 166.7 lbs.

Metric Weight: 75.6 kg

Possible Moves: Future Sight, Nasty Plot, Nightmare, Switcheroo, Pound, Hypnosis, Disable, Confusion, Poison Gas, Meditate, Psybeam, Headbutt, Psych Up, Synchronoise, Zen Headbutt, Swagger, Psychic, Psyshock

Hypno's habit of sending everyone it meets to sleep so it can taste their dreams makes it a dangerous Pokémon—but if you're exhausted and having trouble sleeping, it could be a big help.

EVOLUTION

Drowzee → Hypno

IGGLYBUFF

Balloon Pokémon

How to Say It: IG-lee-buff

Type: Normal-Fairy

Imperial Height: 1'00"

Metric Height: 0.3 m

Imperial Weight: 2.2 lbs.

Metric Weight: 1.0 kg

Possible Moves: Sing, Charm, Defense Curl, Pound, Sweet Kiss, Copycat

Though Igglybuff is an enthusiastic singer, it's not particularly skilled yet. Its bouncing movement causes it to sweat, but fortunately this makes it smell better, not worse.

EVOLUTION

Igglybuff → Jigglypuff → Wigglytuff

INCINEROAR

Heel Pokémon

How to Say It:
in-SIN-uh-roar

Type: Fire-Dark

Imperial Height: 5'11"

Metric Height: 1.8 m

Imperial Weight: 183.0 lbs.

Metric Weight: 83.0 kg

Possible Moves: Darkest Lariat, Bulk Up, Throat Chop, Scratch, Ember, Growl, Lick, Leer, Fire Fang, Roar, Bite, Swagger, Fury Swipes, Thrash, Flamethrower, Scary Face, Flare Blitz, Outrage, Cross Chop

Training an Incineroar requires patience—if it's not in just the right mood, it shows complete disregard for any orders given. During battle, it throws fierce punches and kicks, then launches the flames on its belly in a final attack.

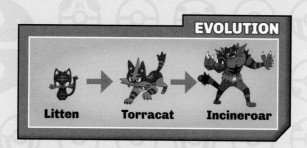

EVOLUTION

Litten → Torracat → Incineroar

JANGMO-O

Scaly Pokémon

How to Say It:
JANG-MOH-oh

Type: Dragon

Imperial Height: 2'00"

Metric Height: 0.6 m

Imperial Weight: 65.5 lbs.

Metric Weight: 29.7 kg

Possible Moves: Tackle, Leer, Bide, Protect, Dragon Tail, Scary Face, Headbutt, Work Up, Screech, Iron Defense, Dragon Claw, Noble Roar, Dragon Dance, Outrage

Wild Jangmo-o live in remote mountains, far away from people. When they smack their scales together, either in battle or to communicate, the mountains ring with the metallic sound.

EVOLUTION

Jangmo-o → Hakamo-o → Kommo-o

JIGGLYPUFF

Balloon Pokémon

How to Say It: JIG-lee-puff

Type: Normal-Fairy

Imperial Height: 1'08"

Metric Height: 0.5 m

Imperial Weight: 12.1 lbs.

Metric Weight: 5.5 kg

Possible Moves: Sing, Defense Curl, Pound, Play Nice, Disarming Voice, Disable, Double Slap, Rollout, Round, Stockpile, Swallow, Spit Up, Wake-Up Slap, Rest, Body Slam, Gyro Ball, Mimic, Hyper Voice, Double-Edge

Because it can inflate its body like a balloon, Jigglypuff has incredible lung capacity. This allows it to sustain its mysterious song until everyone listening falls asleep.

EVOLUTION

Igglybuff → Jigglypuff → Wigglytuff

JOLTEON

Lightning Pokémon

How to Say It: JOL-tee-on

Type: Electric

Imperial Height: 2'07"

Metric Height: 0.8 m

Imperial Weight: 54.0 lbs.

Metric Weight: 24.5 kg

Possible Moves: Thunder Shock, Helping Hand, Tackle, Tail Whip, Sand Attack, Baby-Doll Eyes, Quick Attack, Double Kick, Thunder Fang, Pin Missile, Agility, Thunder Wave, Discharge, Last Resort, Thunder

When Jolteon's fur bristles up, don't stand too close—it might be about to call down a lightning strike! Becoming friends with this Pokémon can be difficult because of its high-strung nature.

EVOLUTION

Eevee → Jolteon

KADABRA

Psi Pokémon

How to Say It:
kuh-DAB-ra

Type: Psychic

Imperial Height: 4'03"

Metric Height: 1.3 m

Imperial Weight: 124.6 lbs.

Metric Weight: 56.5 kg

Possible Moves: Kinesis, Teleport, Confusion, Disable, Psybeam, Miracle Eye, Reflect, Psycho Cut, Recover, Telekinesis, Ally Switch, Psychic, Role Play, Future Sight, Trick

When Kadabra is around, its strong psychic powers can sometimes interfere with electronics like computer monitors or televisions. Strange, creepy shadows can be seen on the screen when this happens.

EVOLUTION

Abra → Kadabra → Alakazam

KANGASKHAN

Parent Pokémon

How to Say It: KANG-gas-con

Type: Normal

Imperial Height: 7'03"

Metric Height: 2.2 m

Imperial Weight: 176.4 lbs.

Metric Weight: 80.0 kg

Possible Moves: Comet Punch, Leer, Fake Out, Tail Whip, Bite, Double Hit, Rage, Mega Punch, Chip Away, Dizzy Punch, Crunch, Endure, Outrage, Sucker Punch, Reversal

Kangaskhan will risk everything to protect the little one in its pouch. If you hear this Pokémon crying, keep an eye out for a young Kangaskhan who's just set out on its own.

EVOLUTION
Does not evolve.

KARTANA

Drawn Sword Pokémon

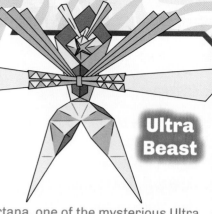

Ultra Beast

How to Say It: kar-TAH-nuh

Type: Grass-Steel

Imperial Height: 1'00"

Metric Height: 0.3 m

Imperial Weight: 0.2 lbs.

Metric Weight: 0.1 kg

Possible Moves: Sacred Sword, Defog, Vacuum Wave, Air Cutter, Fury Cutter, Cut, False Swipe, Razor Leaf, Synthesis, Aerial Ace, Laser Focus, Night Slash, Swords Dance, Leaf Blade, X-Scissor, Detect, Air Slash, Psycho Cut, Guillotine

Kartana, one of the mysterious Ultra Beasts, can use its entire sharp-edged body as a weapon in battle. Its blade is strong and sharp enough to slice right through a steel structure in a single stroke.

EVOLUTION
Does not evolve.

KLEFKI

Key Ring Pokémon

How to Say It: KLEF-key

Type: Steel-Fairy

Imperial Height: 0'08"

Metric Height: 0.2 m

Imperial Weight: 6.6 lbs.

Metric Weight: 3.0 kg

Possible Moves: Fairy Lock, Tackle, Fairy Wind, Astonish, Metal Sound, Spikes, Draining Kiss, Crafty Shield, Foul Play, Torment, Mirror Shot, Imprison, Recycle, Play Rough, Magic Room, Heal Block

If you're constantly losing your keys, a Klefki might be to blame. This Pokémon loves to collect keys and sometimes even swipes them from people's homes.

EVOLUTION
Does not evolve.

KOMALA

Drowsing Pokémon

How to Say It: koh-MAH-luh

Type: Normal

Imperial Height: 1'04"

Metric Height: 0.4 m

Imperial Weight: 43.9 lbs.

Metric Weight: 19.9 kg

Possible Moves: Defense Curl, Rollout, Stockpile, Spit Up, Swallow, Rapid Spin, Yawn, Slam, Flail, Sucker Punch, Psych Up, Wood Hammer, Thrash

Komala never wakes up—ever—although it does sometimes move around as it dreams. It lives in a permanent state of sleep, cuddling its precious log or its Trainer's arm.

EVOLUTION
Does not evolve.

KOMMO-O

Scaly Pokémon

How to Say It: koh-MOH-oh

Type: Dragon-Fighting

Imperial Height: 5'03"

Metric Height: 1.6 m

Imperial Weight: 172.4 lbs.

Metric Weight: 78.2 kg

Possible Moves: Clanging Scales, Sky Uppercut, Belly Drum, Autotomize, Tackle, Leer, Bide, Protect, Dragon Tail, Scary Face, Headbutt, Work Up, Screech, Iron Defense, Dragon Claw, Noble Roar, Dragon Dance, Outrage

Long ago, Kommo-o scales were collected and turned into weapons. For this Pokémon, the scales provide offense, defense, and even a warning system—when it shakes its tail, the scales clash together in a jangle that scares off weak opponents.

EVOLUTION

Jangmo-o   Hakamo-o   Kommo-o

KROKOROK

Desert Croc Pokémon

How to Say It: KRAHK-oh-rahk

Type: Ground-Dark

Imperial Height: 3'03"

Metric Height: 1.0 m

Imperial Weight: 73.6 lbs.

Metric Weight: 33.4 kg

Possible Moves: Leer, Rage, Bite, Sand Attack, Torment, Sand Tomb, Assurance, Mud-Slap, Embargo, Swagger, Crunch, Dig, Scary Face, Foul Play, Sandstorm, Earthquake, Thrash

The membrane that covers Krokorok's eyes keeps sand out and allows it to see even on a dark night. They tend to live in small groups, often led by a female Krokorok.

EVOLUTION

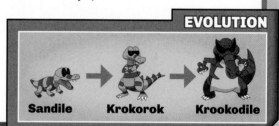

Sandile → Krokorok → Krookodile

KROOKODILE

Intimidation Pokémon

How to Say It: KROOK-oh-dyle

Type: Ground-Dark

Imperial Height: 4'11"

Metric Height: 1.5 m

Imperial Weight: 212.3 lbs.

Metric Weight: 96.3 kg

Possible Moves: Power Trip, Leer, Rage, Bite, Sand Attack, Torment, Sand Tomb, Assurance, Mud-Slap, Embargo, Swagger, Crunch, Dig, Scary Face, Foul Play, Sandstorm, Earthquake, Outrage

With its strong jaws, Krookodile can clamp on to its opponent. With its sharp eyes, it can spot a potential threat—or something it wants to eat—from many miles away, even in a raging sandstorm.

EVOLUTION

Sandile → Krokorok → Krookodile

LANTURN

Light Pokémon

How to Say It: LAN-turn

Type: Water-Electric

Imperial Height: 3'11"

Metric Height: 1.2 m

Imperial Weight: 49.6 lbs.

Metric Weight: 22.5 kg

Possible Moves: Stockpile, Swallow, Spit Up, Eerie Impulse, Bubble, Supersonic, Thunder Wave, Electro Ball, Water Gun, Confuse Ray, Bubble Beam, Spark, Signal Beam, Flail, Discharge, Take Down, Aqua Ring, Hydro Pump, Ion Deluge, Charge

With the bright light from its antennae, Lanturn can blind and daze its opponent, then attack with electricity before it recovers. At night, the lights of many Lanturn shine through the dark ocean like stars.

EVOLUTION

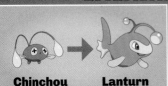

Chinchou → Lanturn

LAPRAS

Transport Pokémon

How to Say It: LAP-rus

Type: Water-Ice

Imperial Height: 8'02"

Metric Height: 2.5 m

Imperial Weight: 485.0 lbs.

Metric Weight: 220.0 kg

Possible Moves: Sing, Growl, Water Gun, Mist, Confuse Ray, Ice Shard, Water Pulse, Body Slam, Rain Dance, Perish Song, Ice Beam, Brine, Safeguard, Hydro Pump, Sheer Cold

Lapras were once nearly wiped out by human activity, but thanks to legal protection, these friendly and intelligent Pokémon are now flourishing. Their lovely singing voices can often be heard near the water when they're having a good day.

EVOLUTION
Does not evolve.

LEAFEON

Verdant Pokémon

How to Say It: LEAF-ee-on

Type: Grass

Imperial Height: 3'03"

Metric Height: 1.0 m

Imperial Weight: 56.2 lbs.

Metric Weight: 25.5 kg

Possible Moves: Razor Leaf, Helping Hand, Tackle, Tail Whip, Sand Attack, Baby-Doll Eyes, Quick Attack, Grass Whistle, Magical Leaf, Giga Drain, Swords Dance, Synthesis, Sunny Day, Last Resort, Leaf Blade

Leafeon doesn't need to eat, because it uses photosynthesis to generate energy. A newly evolved Leafeon smells fresh and green, like spring grass, while an older one wafts the dry, crisp scent of autumn leaves.

EVOLUTION

Eevee → Leafeon

LEDIAN

Five Star Pokémon

How to Say It: LEH-dee-an

Type: Bug-Flying

Imperial Height: 4'07"

Metric Height: 1.4 m

Imperial Weight: 78.5 lbs.

Metric Weight: 35.6 kg

Possible Moves: Tackle, Supersonic, Swift, Light Screen, Reflect, Safeguard, Mach Punch, Silver Wind, Comet Punch, Baton Pass, Agility, Bug Buzz, Air Slash, Double-Edge

Ledian are thought to consume starlight for food, but they're also happy to gobble down berries. They pummel their opponents with all four arms in battle, hoping to overcome the foe with a flurry of punches.

EVOLUTION

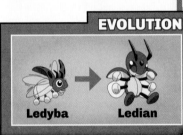

Ledyba → Ledian

LEDYBA

Five Star Pokémon

How to Say It: LEH-dee-bah

Type: Bug-Flying

Imperial Height: 3'03"

Metric Height: 1.0 m

Imperial Weight: 23.8 lbs.

Metric Weight: 10.8 kg

Possible Moves: Tackle, Supersonic, Swift, Light Screen, Reflect, Safeguard, Mach Punch, Silver Wind, Comet Punch, Baton Pass, Agility, Bug Buzz, Air Slash, Double-Edge

Ledyba prefer to stick together, forming brightly patterned swarms. They communicate through scent, and the aromatic fluid they give off changes according to their emotion—a swarm of angry Ledyba smells unpleasantly sour.

EVOLUTION

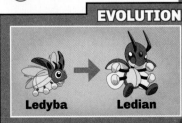

Ledyba → Ledian

LILLIGANT

Flowering Pokémon

How to Say It: LIL-lih-gunt

Type: Grass

Imperial Height: 3'07"

Metric Height: 1.1 m

Imperial Weight: 35.9 lbs.

Metric Weight: 16.3 kg

Possible Moves: Growth, Leech Seed, Mega Drain, Synthesis, Teeter Dance, Quiver Dance, Petal Dance, Petal Blizzard

Some Trainers lavish time, attention, and money on Lilligant, attempting to cultivate its lovely flowers—but this Pokémon always blooms most beautifully when it's left alone in the wild. The showy flowers might be an attempt to attract a partner.

EVOLUTION

Petilil → **Lilligant**

LILLIPUP

Puppy Pokémon

How to Say It: LIL-ee-pup

Type: Normal

Imperial Height: 1'04"

Metric Height: 0.4 m

Imperial Weight: 9.0 lbs.

Metric Weight: 4.1 kg

Possible Moves: Leer, Tackle, Odor Sleuth, Bite, Baby-Doll Eyes, Helping Hand, Take Down, Work Up, Crunch, Roar, Retaliate, Reversal, Last Resort, Giga Impact, Play Rough

The quiet, well-behaved Lillipup is a popular partner for Trainers who live in apartments and have to avoid disturbing their neighbors. Its fluffy facial fur acts as a sensor in battle.

EVOLUTION

Lillipup → **Herdier** → **Stoutland**

LITTEN

Fire Cat Pokémon

How to Say It: LIT-n

Type: Fire

Imperial Height: 1'04"

Metric Height: 0.4 m

Imperial Weight: 9.5 lbs.

Metric Weight: 4.3 kg

Possible Moves: Scratch, Ember, Growl, Lick, Leer, Fire Fang, Roar, Bite, Swagger, Fury Swipes, Thrash, Flamethrower, Scary Face, Flare Blitz, Outrage

When it grooms its fur, Litten is storing up ammunition—the flaming fur is later coughed up in a fiery attack. Trainers often have a hard time getting this solitary Pokémon to trust them.

EVOLUTION

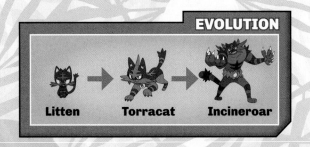

Litten → Torracat → Incineroar

LUCARIO

Aura Pokémon

How to Say It: loo-CAR-ee-oh

Type: Fighting-Steel

Imperial Height: 3'11"

Metric Height: 1.2 m

Imperial Weight: 119.0 lbs.

Metric Weight: 54.0 kg

Possible Moves: Aura Sphere, Laser Focus, Foresight, Quick Attack, Detect, Metal Claw, Counter, Feint, Power-Up Punch, Swords Dance, Metal Sound, Bone Rush, Quick Guard, Me First, Work Up, Calm Mind, Heal Pulse, Close Combat, Dragon Pulse, Extreme Speed

When Lucario evolves, it gains the power not just to sense auras, but to control them. This skill is often useful in battle. If a person or Pokémon within a half-mile radius is feeling happy or sad, Lucario can tell.

EVOLUTION

Riolu → Lucario

LUMINEON

Neon Pokémon

How to Say It: loo-MIN-ee-on

Type: Water

Imperial Height: 3'11"

Metric Height: 1.2 m

Imperial Weight: 52.9 lbs.

Metric Weight: 24.0 kg

Possible Moves: Soak, Pound, Water Gun, Attract, Rain Dance, Gust, Water Pulse, Captivate, Safeguard, Aqua Ring, Whirlpool, U-turn, Bounce, Silver Wind, Soak

In the depths of the sea, Lumineon's body gives off light to attract food—but sometimes bigger Pokémon are attracted to the light instead, and it finds itself in an intense battle.

EVOLUTION

Finneon → Lumineon

LUNALA

Moone Pokémon

How to Say It:
loo-NAH-luh

Type: Psychic-Ghost

Imperial Height: 13'01"

Metric Height: 4.0 m

Imperial Weight: 264.6 lbs.

Metric Weight: 120.0 kg

Legendary Pokémon

Possible Moves: Moongeist Beam, Cosmic Power, Hypnosis, Teleport, Confusion, Night Shade, Confuse Ray, Air Slash, Shadow Ball, Moonlight, Night Daze, Magic Coat, Moonblast, Dream Eater, Phantom Force, Wide Guard, Hyper Beam

Lunala's wide wings soak up the light, plunging the brightest day into shadow. This Legendary Pokémon apparently makes its home in another world, and it returns there when its third eye becomes active.

EVOLUTION

Cosmog → Cosmoem → Lunala

LURANTIS

Bloom Sickle Pokémon

How to Say It:
loor-RAN-tis

Type: Grass

Imperial Height: 2'11"

Metric Height: 0.9 m

Imperial Weight: 40.8 lbs.

Metric Weight: 18.5 kg

Possible Moves: Petal Blizzard, X-Scissor, Fury Cutter, Leafage, Razor Leaf, Growth, Ingrain, Leaf Blade, Synthesis, Slash, Sweet Scent, Solar Blade, Sunny Day

It can be difficult to give Lurantis the proper care to keep its coloring bright and vivid, but some Trainers enthusiastically accept the challenge. The beams it shoots from its petals can pierce thick metal.

EVOLUTION

Fomantis → **Lurantis**

LUVDISC

Rendezvous Pokémon

How to Say It: LOVE-disk

Type: Water

Imperial Height: 2'00"

Metric Height: 0.6 m

Imperial Weight: 19.2 lbs.

Metric Weight: 8.7 kg

Possible Moves: Tackle, Charm, Water Gun, Agility, Draining Kiss, Lucky Chant, Water Pulse, Attract, Heart Stamp, Flail, Sweet Kiss, Take Down, Captivate, Aqua Ring, Soak, Hydro Pump, Safeguard

If you see many Luvdisc swimming in a hotel pool, it's likely the hotel is popular among couples on honeymoon. This Pokémon grows very sad if it's left alone, which can be a huge disadvantage in battle.

EVOLUTION
Does not evolve.

LYCANROC

Wolf Pokémon

Midnight Form

Midday Form

How to Say It: LIE-can-rock

Type: Rock

Imperial Height: Midday Form: 2'07" / Midnight Form: 3'07"

Metric Height: Midday Form: 0.8 m / Midnight Form: 1.1 m

Imperial Weight: 55.1 lbs.

Metric Weight: 25.0 kg

Possible Moves: Tackle, Leer, Sand Attack, Bite, Howl, Rock Throw, Odor Sleuth, Rock Tomb, Roar, Stealth Rock, Rock Slide, Scary Face, Crunch, Rock Climb, Stone Edge

Midday Form: Accelerock, Quick Guard, Quick Attack

Midnight Form: Counter, Reversal, Taunt

Its thick mane conceals sharp rocks that it uses in battle along with its fangs and claws. Despite its fearsome arsenal, Lycanroc displays fierce loyalty toward a Trainer who has raised it well.

EVOLUTION

Rockruff → Lycanroc Midday Form

Rockruff → Lycanroc Midnight Form

MACHAMP

Superpower Pokémon

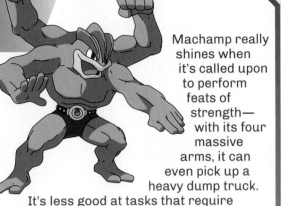

How to Say It: muh-CHAMP

Type: Fighting

Imperial Height: 5'03"

Metric Height: 1.6 m

Imperial Weight: 286.6 lbs.

Metric Weight: 130.0 kg

Possible Moves: Strength, Wide Guard, Low Kick, Leer, Focus Energy, Karate Chop, Foresight, Low Sweep, Seismic Toss, Revenge, Knock Off, Vital Throw, Wake-Up Slap, Dual Chop, Submission, Bulk Up, Cross Chop, Scary Face, Dynamic Punch

Machamp really shines when it's called upon to perform feats of strength— with its four massive arms, it can even pick up a heavy dump truck. It's less good at tasks that require manual dexterity and precision.

EVOLUTION

Machop → Machoke → Machamp

MACHOKE

Superpower Pokémon

How to Say It: muh-CHOKE

Type: Fighting

Imperial Height: 4'11"

Metric Height: 1.5 m

Imperial Weight: 155.4 lbs.

Metric Weight: 70.5 kg

Possible Moves: Low Kick, Leer, Focus Energy, Karate Chop, Foresight, Low Sweep, Seismic Toss, Revenge, Knock Off, Vital Throw, Wake-Up Slap, Dual Chop, Submission, Bulk Up, Cross Chop, Scary Face, Dynamic Punch

Machoke happily pitches in when people need help with a tough physical job. Moving and carrying heavy things is just one more way for it to train its muscles.

EVOLUTION

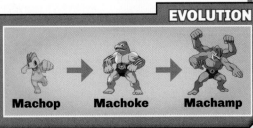

Machop → Machoke → Machamp

MACHOP

Superpower Pokémon

How to Say It: muh-CHOP

Type: Fighting

Imperial Height: 2'07"

Metric Height: 0.8 m

Imperial Weight: 43.0 lbs.

Metric Weight: 19.5 kg

Possible Moves: Low Kick, Leer, Focus Energy, Karate Chop, Foresight, Low Sweep, Seismic Toss, Revenge, Knock Off, Vital Throw, Wake-Up Slap, Dual Chop, Submission, Bulk Up, Cross Chop, Scary Face, Dynamic Punch

Exercise is Machop's favorite thing in the world, and its developing muscles reinforce its devotion to working out. It's strong enough to pick up and throw the weight of a hundred people.

EVOLUTION

Machop → Machoke → Machamp

MAGBY

Live Coal Pokémon

How to Say It: MAG-bee

Type: Fire

Imperial Height: 2'04"

Metric Height: 0.7 m

Imperial Weight: 47.2 lbs.

Metric Weight: 21.4 kg

Possible Moves: Smog, Leer, Ember, Smokescreen, Feint Attack, Fire Spin, Clear Smog, Flame Burst, Confuse Ray, Fire Punch, Lava Plume, Sunny Day, Flamethrower, Fire Blast

Magby thrive in volcanic areas, where they can freely spout flames. They can learn to control their flames and use them productively— for instance, one Magby serves as a gentle kiln for its Trainer, an artist famous for pottery.

EVOLUTION

Magby → Magmar → Magmortar

MAGEARNA

Artificial Pokémon

Mythical Pokémon

How to Say It:
muh-GEER-nuh

Type: Steel-Fairy

Imperial Height: 3'03"

Metric Height: 1.0 m

Imperial Weight: 177.5 lbs.

Metric Weight: 80.5 kg

Possibles Moves: Crafty Shield, Gear Up, Shift Gear, Iron Head, Helping Hand, Sonic Boom, Defense Curl, Psybeam, Lucky Chant, Aurora Beam, Mirror Shot, Mind Reader, Flash Cannon, Fleur Cannon, Iron Defense, Pain Split, Synchronoise, Aura Sphere, Heart Swap, Trump Card

Magearna was built many centuries ago by human inventors. The rest of this Pokémon's mechanical body is just a vehicle for its true self: the Soul-Heart contained in its chest.

EVOLUTION
Does not evolve.

MAGIKARP

Fish Pokémon

How to Say It:
MADGE-eh-karp

Type: Water

Imperial Height: 2'11"

Metric Height: 0.9 m

Imperial Weight: 22.0 lbs.

Metric Weight: 10.0 kg

Possible Moves: Splash, Tackle, Flail

Magikarp splash about with abandon, leaping recklessly out of the water—which leaves them open to attack. Though extremely lacking when it comes to battle strength, they exist in huge numbers.

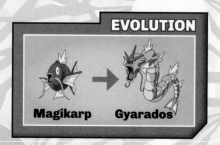

EVOLUTION

Magikarp → Gyarados

MAGMAR

Spitfire Pokémon

How to Say It:
MAG-marr

Type: Fire

Imperial Height:
4'03"

Metric Height: 1.3 m

Imperial Weight: 98.1 lbs.

Metric Weight: 44.5 kg

Possible Moves: Smog,
Leer, Ember, Smokescreen,
Feint Attack, Fire Spin, Clear
Smog, Flame Burst, Confuse
Ray, Fire Punch, Lava Plume,
Sunny Day, Flamethrower,
Fire Blast

Taking a hot bath is a great way for some people to recharge. Magmar likes to do that, too—but instead of hot water, it bathes in molten lava! Flames spout from its body in battle.

EVOLUTION

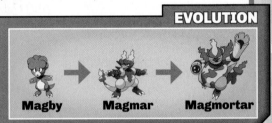

Magby → **Magmar** → **Magmortar**

MAGMORTAR

Blast Pokémon

How to Say It: mag-MORT-ur

Type: Fire

Imperial Height: 5'03"

Metric Height: 1.6 m

Imperial Weight:
149.9 lbs.

Metric Weight: 68.0 kg

Possible Moves: Thunder
Punch, Smog, Leer, Ember,
Smokescreen, Feint Attack,
Fire Spin, Clear Smog, Flame
Burst, Confuse Ray, Fire
Punch, Lava Plume, Sunny
Day, Flamethrower, Fire Blast,
Hyper Beam

Magmortar can shoot balls of fire out of its arm, although it has to avoid firing several at once—the buildup of such intense heat can cause melting. Apparently, each pair of Magmortar claims a separate volcano as home.

EVOLUTION

Magby → **Magmar** → **Magmortar**

MAGNEMITE

Magnet Pokémon

How to Say It: MAG-ne-mite

Type: Electric-Steel

Imperial Height: 1'00"

Metric Height: 0.3 m

Imperial Weight: 13.2 lbs.

Metric Weight: 6.0 kg

Possible Moves: Tackle, Supersonic, Thunder Shock, Magnet Bomb, Thunder Wave, Light Screen, Sonic Boom, Spark, Mirror Shot, Metal Sound, Electro Ball, Flash Cannon, Screech, Discharge, Lock-On, Magnet Rise, Gyro Ball, Zap Cannon

Groups of Magnemite often cluster around transmission towers to suck up electricity from the power lines. They float above the ground by using electromagnetic waves.

EVOLUTION

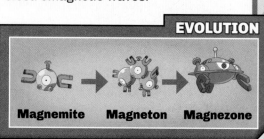

Magnemite   Magneton   Magnezone

MAGNETON

Magnet Pokémon

How to Say It: MAG-ne-ton

Type: Electric-Steel

Imperial Height: 3'03"

Metric Height: 1.0 m

Imperial Weight: 132.3 lbs.

Metric Weight: 60.0 kg

Possible Moves: Tri Attack, Zap Cannon, Electric Terrain, Tackle, Supersonic, Thunder Shock, Magnet Bomb, Thunder Wave, Light Screen, Sonic Boom, Spark, Mirror Shot, Metal Sound, Electro Ball, Flash Cannon, Screech, Discharge, Lock-On, Magnet Rise, Gyro Ball

Magneton is formed when three Magnemite link their bodies and brains together. This triples their electrical power, but their intelligence doesn't get a similar boost.

EVOLUTION

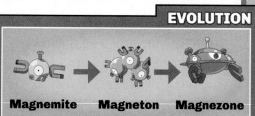

Magnemite   Magneton   Magnezone

MAGNEZONE

Magnet Area Pokémon

How to Say It: MAG-nuh-zone

Type: Electric-Steel

Imperial Height: 3'11"

Metric Height: 1.2 m

Imperial Weight: 396.8 lbs.

Metric Weight: 180.0 kg

Possible Moves: Tri Attack, Zap Cannon, Magnetic Flux, Mirror Coat, Barrier, Electric Terrain, Tackle, Supersonic, Thunder Shock, Magnet Bomb, Thunder Wave, Light Screen, Sonic Boom, Spark, Mirror Shot, Metal Sound, Electro Ball, Flash Cannon, Screech, Discharge, Lock-On, Magnet Rise, Gyro Ball

Magnezone is thought to receive and transmit signals as it flies through the air with the power of magnetism, though it's unknown where the signals come from. Sometimes a reported UFO sighting turns out to be Magnezone.

EVOLUTION

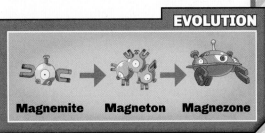

Magnemite → **Magneton** → **Magnezone**

MAKUHITA

Guts Pokémon

How to Say It: MAK-oo-HEE-ta

Type: Fighting

Imperial Height: 3'03"

Metric Height: 1.0 m

Imperial Weight: 190.5 lbs.

Metric Weight: 86.4 kg

Possible Moves: Tackle, Focus Energy, Sand Attack, Arm Thrust, Fake Out, Force Palm, Whirlwind, Knock Off, Vital Throw, Belly Drum, Smelling Salts, Seismic Toss, Wake-Up Slap, Endure, Close Combat, Reversal, Heavy Slam

Makuhita aren't native to the Alola region, but they've definitely made a name for themselves in the islands. Groups of Makuhita gather every day for training, eating, napping, and more training.

EVOLUTION

Makuhita → **Hariyama**

MANDIBUZZ

Bone Vulture Pokémon

How to Say It: MAN-dih-buz

Type: Dark-Flying

Imperial Height: 3'11"

Metric Height: 1.2 m

Imperial Weight: 87.1 lbs.

Metric Weight: 39.5 kg

Possible Moves: Bone Rush, Mirror Move, Brave Bird, Whirlwind, Gust, Leer, Fury Attack, Pluck, Nasty Plot, Flatter, Feint Attack, Punishment, Defog, Tailwind, Air Slash, Dark Pulse, Embargo

Mandibuzz weave bones into their feathers and wear them as jewelry, perhaps in an attempt to show off. They fly in circles, always keeping an eye out for a weaker opponent down below.

EVOLUTION

Vullaby → Mandibuzz

MANKEY

Pig Monkey Pokémon

How to Say It: MANG-key

Type: Fighting

Imperial Height: 1'08"

Metric Height: 0.5 m

Imperial Weight: 61.7 lbs.

Metric Weight: 28.0 kg

Possible Moves: Covet, Scratch, Low Kick, Leer, Focus Energy, Fury Swipes, Karate Chop, Pursuit, Seismic Toss, Swagger, Cross Chop, Assurance, Punishment, Thrash, Close Combat, Screech, Stomping Tantrum, Outrage, Final Gambit

Mankey's rage is so exhausting that it falls asleep, then wakes itself up by rampaging through its dreams—and waking up makes it mad! Being lonely makes it angry, but its rage drives everyone away—and then it's lonely again!

EVOLUTION

Mankey → Primeape

MAREANIE

Brutal Star Pokémon

How to Say It:
muh-REE-nee

Type: Poison-Water

Imperial Height: 1'04"

Metric Height: 0.4 m

Imperial Weight: 17.6 lbs.

Metric Weight: 8.0 kg

Possible Moves: Poison Sting, Peck, Bite, Toxic Spikes, Wide Guard, Toxic, Venoshock, Spike Cannon, Recover, Poison Jab, Venom Drench, Pin Missile, Liquidation

Mareanie lives at the bottom of the sea or along the beach. It attacks with its head spike, which delivers poison that can weaken a foe. It's often tempted by the brightly colored coral of Corsola.

EVOLUTION

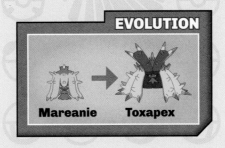

Mareanie   →   Toxapex

MAROWAK (Alola Form)

Bone Keeper Pokémon

The flaming bone that Marowak spins like a baton once belonged to its mother, and it's protected by its mother's spirit. It grieves for its fallen companions, visiting their graves along the roadside.

How to Say It:
MARE-oh-wack

Type: Fire-Ghost

Imperial Height: 3'03"

Metric Height: 1.0 m

Imperial Weight: 75.0 lbs.

Metric Weight: 34.0 kg

Possible Moves: Growl, Tail Whip, Bone Club, Flame Wheel, Leer, Hex, Bonemerang, Will-O-Wisp, Shadow Bone, Thrash, Fling, Stomping Tantrum, Endeavor, Double-Edge, Retaliate, Bone Rush, Flare Blitz

EVOLUTION

Cubone → Marowak

MASQUERAIN

Eyeball Pokémon

How to Say It: mas-ker-RAIN

Type: Bug-Flying

Imperial Height: 2'07"

Metric Height: 0.8 m

Imperial Weight: 7.9 lbs.

Metric Weight: 3.6 kg

Possible Moves: Quiver Dance, Whirlwind, Bug Buzz, Ominous Wind, Bubble, Quick Attack, Sweet Scent, Water Sport, Gust, Scary Face, Air Cutter, Stun Spore, Silver Wind, Air Slash

The eye patterns on Masquerain's large antennae sometimes scare away foes. Its four tiny wings enable it to dart around in any direction, though they can get waterlogged in the rain.

EVOLUTION

Surskit → Masquerain

MEOWTH (Alola Form)

Scratch Cat Pokémon

How to Say It: mee-OWTH

Type: Dark

Imperial Height: 1'04"

Metric Height: 0.4 m

Imperial Weight: 9.3 lbs.

Metric Weight: 4.2 kg

Possible Moves: Scratch, Growl, Bite, Fake Out, Fury Swipes, Screech, Feint Attack, Taunt, Pay Day, Slash, Nasty Plot, Assurance, Captivate, Night Slash, Feint, Dark Pulse

Meowth is very vain about the golden Charm on its forehead, becoming enraged if any dirt dulls its bright surface. These crafty Pokémon are not native to Alola, but thanks to human interference, their population has surged.

EVOLUTION

Meowth → Persian

METAGROSS

Iron Leg Pokémon

How to Say It: MET-uh-gross

Type: Steel-Psychic

Imperial Height: 5'03"

Metric Height: 1.6 m

Imperial Weight: 1,212.5 lbs.

Metric Weight: 550.0 kg

Possible Moves: Hammer Arm, Confusion, Metal Claw, Magnet Rise, Take Down, Pursuit, Bullet Punch, Miracle Eye, Zen Headbutt, Scary Face, Psychic, Agility, Meteor Mash, Iron Defense, Hyper Beam

Metagross is formed when two Metang combine. It is intimidating both physically and mentally—it can easily pin a foe underneath its massive steel body, and its four brains perform complicated calculations in the blink of an eye.

EVOLUTION

Beldum → Metang → Metagross

METANG

Iron Claw Pokémon

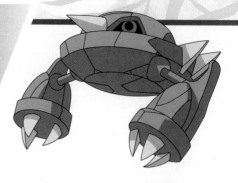

How to Say It: met-TANG

Type: Steel-Psychic

Imperial Height: 3'11"

Metric Height: 1.2 m

Imperial Weight: 446.4 lbs.

Metric Weight: 202.5 kg

Possible Moves: Confusion, Metal Claw, Magnet Rise, Take Down, Pursuit, Bullet Punch, Miracle Eye, Zen Headbutt, Scary Face, Psychic, Agility, Meteor Mash, Iron Defense, Hyper Beam

Metang is formed when two Beldum combine. This doubles their psychic power but does not boost their intelligence. Metang is always seeking magnetic minerals and is particularly drawn to Nosepass.

EVOLUTION

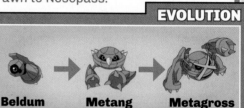

Beldum → Metang → Metagross

METAPOD

Cocoon Pokémon

How to Say It: MET-uh-pod

Type: Bug

Imperial Height: 2'04"

Metric Height: 0.7 m

Imperial Weight: 21.8 lbs.

Metric Weight: 9.9 kg

Possible Move: Harden

Inside Metapod's hard shell, its body is soft and vulnerable. It takes care not to move around too much or get into serious battles for fear of breaking the shell.

EVOLUTION

Caterpie → Metapod → Butterfree

MILOTIC

Tender Pokémon

How to Say It: MY-low-tic

Type: Water

Imperial Height: 20'04"

Metric Height: 6.2 m

Imperial Weight: 357.1 lbs.

Metric Weight: 162.0 kg

Possible Moves: Water Pulse, Wrap, Water Gun, Water Sport, Refresh, Disarming Voice, Twister, Aqua Ring, Captivate, Dragon Tail, Recover, Aqua Tail, Attract, Safeguard, Coil, Hydro Pump, Rain Dance

Milotic sometimes serves as a muse to artists who wish to capture its astounding beauty in their work. Just looking at this lovely Pokémon can be enough to calm one's nerves or stop a fight.

EVOLUTION

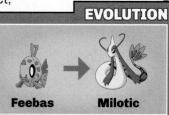

Feebas → Milotic

MILTANK

Milk Cow Pokémon

How to Say It: MILL-tank

Type: Normal

Imperial Height: 3'11"

Metric Height: 1.2 m

Imperial Weight: 166.4 lbs.

Metric Weight: 75.5 kg

Possible Moves: Tackle, Growl, Defense Curl, Stomp, Milk Drink, Bide, Rollout, Body Slam, Zen Headbutt, Captivate, Gyro Ball, Heal Bell, Wake-Up Slap

The milk that Miltank produces is calorie-dense and highly nutritious. Although it's best known for this milk, it can also hold its own in battle thanks to its strength and toughness.

EVOLUTION
Does not evolve.

MIMIKYU

Disguise Pokémon

How to Say It:
MEE-mee-kyoo

Type: Ghost-Fairy

Imperial Height: 0'08"

Metric Height: 0.2 m

Imperial Weight: 1.5 lbs.

Metric Weight: 0.7 kg

Possible Moves: Wood Hammer, Splash, Scratch, Astonish, Copycat, Double Team, Baby-Doll Eyes, Shadow Sneak, Mimic, Feint Attack, Charm, Slash, Shadow Claw, Hone Claws, Play Rough, Pain Split

What does Mimikyu look like? No one really knows, but apparently it's terrifying—it always hides underneath an old rag so it doesn't scare anyone while it's trying to make friends.

EVOLUTION
Does not evolve.

MINIOR

Meteor Pokémon

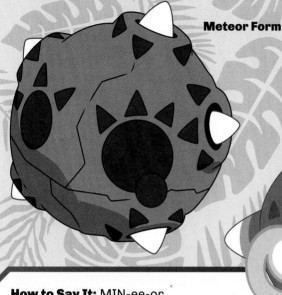

Meteor Form

Red Core Form

How to Say It: MIN-ee-or

Type: Rock-Flying

Imperial Height: Meteor Form: 1'00"/
Red Core Form: 1'00"

Metric Height: Meteor Form: 0.3 m / Red Core Form: 0.3 m

Imperial Weight: Meteor Form: 88.2 lbs. / Red Core Form: 0.7 lbs.

Metric Weight: Meteor Form: 40.0 kg / Red Core Form: 0.3 kg

Possible Moves: Tackle, Defense Curl, Rollout, Confuse Ray, Swift, Ancient Power, Self-Destruct, Stealth Rock, Take Down, Autotomize, Cosmic Power, Power Gem, Double-Edge, Shell Smash, Explosion

Minior came into being when tiny particles in the ozone layer underwent mutation. When its shell becomes too heavy, it falls to the ground, and the impact can knock its shell clean off.

EVOLUTION
Does not evolve.

MISDREAVUS

Screech Pokémon

How to Say It: mis-DREE-vuss

Type: Ghost

Imperial Height: 2'04"

Metric Height: 0.7 m

Imperial Weight: 2.2 lbs.

Metric Weight: 1.0 kg

Possible Moves: Growl, Psywave, Spite, Astonish, Confuse Ray, Mean Look, Hex, Psybeam, Pain Split, Payback, Shadow Ball, Perish Song, Grudge, Power Gem

Misdreavus gets its energy from scaring people and soaking up their fear. One of its favorite tricks is hiding in an otherwise empty room and making a noise that sounds like someone weeping.

EVOLUTION

Misdreavus → Mismagius

MISMAGIUS

Magical Pokémon

How to Say It: miss-MAG-ee-us

Type: Ghost

Imperial Height: 2'11"

Metric Height: 0.9 m

Imperial Weight: 9.7 lbs.

Metric Weight: 4.4 kg

Possible Moves: Mystical Fire, Power Gem, Phantom Force, Lucky Chant, Magical Leaf, Growl, Psywave, Spite, Astonish

Mismagius wields an impressive arsenal of tricks to torment people—launching curses, creating visions of terror, and casting love spells. Some people have been fooled into thinking the last one is harmless fun.

EVOLUTION

Misdreavus → Mismagius

MORELULL

Illuminating Pokémon

How to Say It: MORE-eh-lull

Type: Grass-Fairy

Imperial Height: 0'08"

Metric Height: 0.2 m

Imperial Weight: 3.3 lbs.

Metric Weight: 1.5 kg

Possible Moves: Absorb, Astonish, Flash, Moonlight, Mega Drain, Sleep Powder, Ingrain, Confuse Ray, Giga Drain, Strength Sap, Spore, Moonblast, Dream Eater, Spotlight

The spores that Morelull gives off flicker with a hypnotic light that sends viewers to sleep. During the day, it plants itself beside a tree to absorb nutrients from the roots while it naps.

EVOLUTION

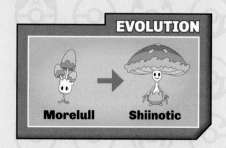

Morelull   Shiinotic

MUDBRAY

Donkey Pokémon

How to Say It: MUD-bray

Type: Ground

Imperial Height: 3'03"

Metric Height: 1.0 m

Imperial Weight: 242.5 lbs.

Metric Weight: 110.0 kg

Possible Moves: Mud-Slap, Mud Sport, Rototiller, Bulldoze, Double Kick, Stomp, Bide, High Horsepower, Iron Defense, Heavy Slam, Counter, Earthquake, Mega Kick, Superpower

Mudbray just loves to get dirty, but it isn't just for fun. Playing in the mud actually gives it better traction for running—when its hooves are covered in dirt, they're less likely to slip, and it can run faster.

EVOLUTION

Mudbray   Mudsdale

MUDSDALE

Draft Horse Pokémon

How to Say It: MUDZ-dale

Type: Ground

Imperial Height: 8'02"

Metric Height: 2.5 m

Imperial Weight: 2,028.3 lbs.

Metric Weight: 920.0 kg

Possible Moves: Mud-Slap, Mud Sport, Rototiller, Bulldoze, Double Kick, Stomp, Bide, High Horsepower, Iron Defense, Heavy Slam, Counter, Earthquake, Mega Kick, Superpower

With the help of the mud that coats its hooves, Mudsdale can deliver heavy kicks powerful enough to demolish a big truck. The mud it produces is weather-resistant, and people used to use it to shore up their houses.

EVOLUTION

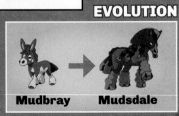

Mudbray   Mudsdale

MUK (Alola Form)

Sludge Pokémon

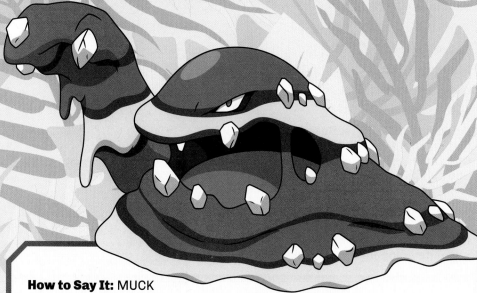

How to Say It: MUCK

Type: Poison-Dark

Imperial Height: 3'03"

Metric Height: 1.0 m

Imperial Weight: 114.6 lbs.

Metric Weight: 52.0 kg

Possible Moves: Venom Drench, Pound, Poison Gas, Harden, Bite, Disable, Acid Spray, Poison Fang, Minimize, Fling, Knock Off, Crunch, Screech, Gunk Shot, Acid Armor, Belch, Memento

Muk's bright and colorful markings are the result of chemical changes in its body, caused by its diet of all sorts of garbage. It's generally a pleasant and friendly companion, but if it gets hungry, it can turn destructive.

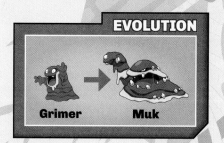

EVOLUTION

Grimer → Muk

MUNCHLAX

Big Eater Pokémon

How to Say It: MUNCH-lax

Type: Normal

Imperial Height: 2'00"

Metric Height: 0.6 m

Imperial Weight: 231.5 lbs.

Metric Weight: 105.0 kg

Possible Moves: Last Resort, Recycle, Lick, Metronome, Odor Sleuth, Tackle, Defense Curl, Amnesia, Lick, Chip Away, Screech, Body Slam, Stockpile, Swallow, Rollout, Fling, Belly Drum, Natural Gift, Snatch

Munchlax has an insatiable appetite, and it isn't too picky about flavors. To sustain itself, it has to keep eating, swallowing just about anything that looks edible.

EVOLUTION

Munchlax → Snorlax

MURKROW

Darkness Pokémon

How to Say It: MUR-crow

Type: Dark-Flying

Imperial Height: 1'08"

Metric Height: 0.5 m

Imperial Weight: 4.6 lbs.

Metric Weight: 2.1 kg

Possible Moves: Peck, Astonish, Pursuit, Haze, Wing Attack, Night Shade, Assurance, Taunt, Feint Attack, Mean Look, Foul Play, Tailwind, Sucker Punch, Torment, Quash

It's unusual to see a Murkrow flying around during the day—they generally sleep until dusk and do their flying at night. They keep an eye out for sparkly objects, which they sometimes offer as a gift to a Trainer.

EVOLUTION

Murkrow → Honchkrow

NECROZMA

Prism Pokémon

How to Say It:
neh-KROHZ-muh

Type: Psychic

Imperial Height: 7'10"

Metric Height: 2.4 m

Imperial Weight: 507.1 lbs.

Metric Weight: 230.0 kg

Possible Moves: Moonlight, Morning Sun, Charge Beam, Mirror Shot, Metal Claw, Confusion, Slash, Stored Power, Rock Blast, Night Slash, Gravity, Psycho Cut, Power Gem, Autotomize, Stealth Rock, Iron Defense, Wring Out, Prismatic Laser

Legendary Pokémon

Some think Necrozma arrived from another world many eons ago. When it emerges from its underground slumber, it seems to absorb light for use as energy to power its laser-like blasts.

EVOLUTION
Does not evolve.

NIHILEGO

Parasite Pokémon

How to Say It: NIE-uh-LEE-go

Type: Rock-Poison

Imperial Height: 3'11"

Metric Height: 1.2 m

Imperial Weight: 122.4 lbs.

Metric Weight: 55.5 kg

Ultra Beast

Possible Moves: Power Split, Guard Split, Tickle, Acid, Constrict, Pound, Clear Smog, Psywave, Headbutt, Venoshock, Toxic Spikes, Safeguard, Power Gem, Mirror Coat, Acid Spray, Venom Drench, Stealth Rock, Wonder Room, Head Smash

Nihilego, one of the mysterious Ultra Beasts, can apparently infest other beings and incite them to violence. Research is inconclusive as to whether this Pokémon can think for itself, but it sometimes exhibits the behavior of a young girl.

EVOLUTION
Does not evolve.

NINETALES (ALOLA FORM)

Fox Pokémon

How to Say It: NINE-tails

Type: Ice-Fairy

Imperial Height: 3'07"

Metric Height: 1.1m

Imperial Weight: 43.9 lbs.

Metric Weight: 19.9kg

Possible Moves: Dazzling Gleam, Imprison, Nasty Plot, Ice Beam, Ice Shard, Confuse Ray, Safeguard

In its frosty coat, Ninetales creates ice droplets that can be used to shower over opponents. It's generally calm and collected, but if it becomes angry, it can freeze the offenders in their tracks.

EVOLUTION

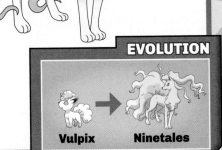

Vulpix → Ninetales

NOSEPASS

Compass Pokémon

How to Say It: NOSE-pass

Type: Rock

Imperial Height: 3'03"

Metric Height: 1.0 m

Imperial Weight: 213.8 lbs.

Metric Weight: 97.0 kg

Possible Moves: Tackle, Harden, Block, Rock Throw, Thunder Wave, Rest, Spark, Rock Slide, Power Gem, Rock Blast, Discharge, Sandstorm, Earth Power, Stone Edge, Lock-On, Zap Cannon

Some Trainers bring along a Nosepass for navigation on their journey, since its magnetic nose serves as a foolproof compass. If the nose attracts metal objects, Nosepass collects them and uses them as a shield.

EVOLUTION

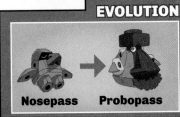

Nosepass → Probopass

ORANGURU

Sage Pokémon

How to Say It:
or-RANG-goo-roo

Type: Normal-Psychic

Imperial Height: 4'11"

Metric Height: 1.5 m

Imperial Weight: 167.6 lbs.

Metric Weight: 76.0 kg

Possible Moves: Confusion, After You, Taunt, Quash, Stored Power, Psych Up, Feint Attack, Nasty Plot, Zen Headbutt, Instruct, Foul Play, Calm Mind, Psychic, Future Sight, Trick Room

Extremely intelligent and somewhat particular, Oranguru can be a bad fit for Trainers who lack experience. In the wild, it spends most of its time in the jungle canopy, though it sometimes emerges in search of an intellectual challenge.

EVOLUTION
Does not evolve.

ORICORIO (BAILE STYLE)

Dancing Pokémon

How to Say It: or-ih-KOR-ee-oh

Type: Fire-Flying

Imperial Height: 2'00"

Metric Height: 0.6 m

Imperial Weight: 7.5 lbs.

Metric Weight: 3.4 kg

Possible Moves: Pound, Growl, Peck, Helping Hand, Air Cutter, Baton Pass, Feather Dance, Double Slap, Teeter Dance, Roost, Captivate, Air Slash, Revelation Dance, Mirror Move, Agility, Hurricane

Drinking red nectar gives Oricorio a fiery style when it dances. It's best to enjoy this beautiful performance from a distance, because its beating wings give off scorching flames.

EVOLUTION
Does not evolve.

ORICORIO (PA'U STYLE)

Dancing Pokémon

How to Say It:
or-ih-KOR-ee-oh

Type: Psychic-Flying

Imperial Height: 2'00"

Metric Height: 0.6 m

Imperial Weight: 7.5 lbs.

Metric Weight: 3.4 kg

Possible Moves: Pound, Growl, Peck, Helping Hand, Air Cutter, Baton Pass, Feather Dance, Double Slap, Teeter Dance, Roost, Captivate, Air Slash, Revelation Dance, Mirror Move, Agility, Hurricane

Drinking pink nectar transforms Oricorio into a hypnotically swaying dancer. As its opponents watch, entranced, the swaying movement relaxes Oricorio's mind so it can build up psychic energy for attacks.

EVOLUTION
Does not evolve.

ORICORIO (POM-POM STYLE)

Dancing Pokémon

How to Say It:
or-ih-KOR-ee-oh

Type: Electric-Flying

Imperial Height: 2'00"

Metric Height: 0.6 m

Imperial Weight: 7.5 lbs.

Metric Weight: 3.4 kg

Possible Moves: Pound, Growl, Peck, Helping Hand, Air Cutter, Baton Pass, Feather Dance, Double Slap, Teeter Dance, Roost, Captivate, Air Slash, Revelation Dance, Mirror Move, Agility, Hurricane

Drinking yellow nectar makes Oricorio's dance style truly electric. The charge generated by the rubbing of its feathers allows it to land truly shocking punches in battle as it performs a cheerful dance.

EVOLUTION
Does not evolve.

ORICORIO (SENSU STYLE)

Dancing Pokémon

How to Say It:
or-ih-KOR-ee-oh

Type: Ghost-Flying

Imperial Height: 2'00"

Metric Height: 0.6 m

Imperial Weight: 7.5 lbs.

Metric Weight: 3.4 kg

Possible Moves: Pound, Growl, Peck, Helping Hand, Air Cutter, Baton Pass, Feather Dance, Double Slap, Teeter Dance, Roost, Captivate, Air Slash, Revelation Dance, Mirror Move, Agility, Hurricane

Drinking purple nectar inspires Oricorio to perform a dreamy and elegant dance. The spirits of the departed are drawn to this beautiful performance, and Oricorio channels their power into its attacks.

EVOLUTION
Does not evolve.

PALOSSAND

Sand Castle Pokémon

How to Say It: PAL-uh-sand

Type: Ghost-Ground

Imperial Height: 4'03"

Metric Height: 1.3 m

Imperial Weight: 551.2 lbs.

Metric Weight: 250.0 kg

Possible Moves: Harden, Absorb, Astonish, Sand Attack, Sand Tomb, Mega Drain, Bulldoze, Hypnosis, Iron Defense, Giga Drain, Shadow Ball, Earth Power, Shore Up, Sandstorm

In order to evolve, this Pokémon took control of people playing in the sand to build up its body into a sand castle. Those who disappear can sometimes be found buried underneath Palossand, drained of their vitality.

EVOLUTION

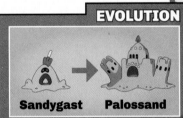

Sandygast   Palossand

PANCHAM

Playful Pokémon

How to Say It: PAN-chum

Type: Fighting

Imperial Height: 2'00"

Metric Height: 0.6 m

Imperial Weight: 17.6 lbs.

Metric Weight: 8.0 kg

Possible Moves: Tackle, Leer, Arm Thrust, Work Up, Karate Chop, Comet Punch, Slash, Circle Throw, Vital Throw, Body Slam, Crunch, Entrainment, Parting Shot, Sky Uppercut

The leaf Pancham holds in its mouth serves no purpose—it's just imitating its hero, Pangoro. Trainers who are beginning their journey could have some trouble handling this mischievous Pokémon.

EVOLUTION

Pancham   Pangoro

PANGORO

Daunting Pokémon

How to Say It: PAN-go-roh

Type: Fighting-Dark

Imperial Height: 6'11"

Metric Height: 2.1 m

Imperial Weight: 299.8 lbs.

Metric Weight: 136.0 kg

Possible Moves: Bullet Punch, Hammer Arm, Low Sweep, Tackle, Leer, Arm Thrust, Work Up, Karate Chop, Comet Punch, Slash, Circle Throw, Vital Throw, Body Slam, Crunch, Entrainment, Parting Shot, Sky Uppercut, Taunt

The bamboo leaf Pangoro keeps in its mouth helps it track its opponent's movements. Its respect for authority is based on battle prowess—a Trainer might have to engage in a test of physical strength before this Pokémon will listen.

EVOLUTION

Pancham → Pangoro

PARAS

Mushroom Pokémon

How to Say It: PAIR-us

Type: Bug-Grass

Imperial Height: 1'00"

Metric Height: 0.3 m

Imperial Weight: 11.9 lbs.

Metric Weight: 5.4 kg

Possible Moves: Scratch, Stun Spore, Poison Powder, Absorb, Fury Cutter, Spore, Slash, Growth, Giga Drain, Aromatherapy, Rage Powder, X-Scissor

When Paras eats, it's mostly just feeding the mushrooms that grow on its back. These mushrooms, known as tochukaso, can be picked, dried, and ground into a powder for use in medicine.

EVOLUTION

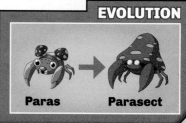

Paras → Parasect

PARASECT

Mushroom Pokémon

How to Say It: PARA-sekt

Type: Bug-Grass

Imperial Height: 3'03"

Metric Height: 1.0 m

Imperial Weight: 65.0 lbs.

Metric Weight: 29.5 kg

Possible Moves: Cross Poison, Scratch, Stun Spore, Poison Powder, Absorb, Fury Cutter, Spore, Slash, Growth, Giga Drain, Aromatherapy, Rage Powder, X-Scissor

Parasect is just a pawn of the giant mushroom that controls it. The mushroom's spores are toxic, but they do have medicinal properties for those careful enough to harvest them safely.

EVOLUTION

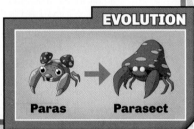

Paras → Parasect

PASSIMIAN

Teamwork Pokémon

How to Say It: pass-SIM-ee-uhn

Type: Fighting

Imperial Height: 6'07"

Metric Height: 2.0 m

Imperial Weight: 182.5 lbs.

Metric Weight: 82.8 kg

Possible Moves: Tackle, Leer, Rock Smash, Focus Energy, Beat Up, Scary Face, Take Down, Bestow, Thrash, Bulk Up, Double-Edge, Fling, Close Combat, Reversal, Giga Impact

Passimian are real team players—they learn from each other and work together for the benefit of the group. Each group, composed of about twenty Passimian, shares a remarkably strong bond.

EVOLUTION
Does not evolve.

PELIPPER

Water Bird Pokémon

How to Say It: PEL-ip-purr

Type: Water-Flying

Imperial Height: 3'11"

Metric Height: 1.2 m

Imperial Weight: 61.7 lbs.

Metric Weight: 28.0 kg

Possible Moves: Protect, Hurricane, Hydro Pump, Tailwind, Soak, Growl, Water Gun, Water Sport, Supersonic, Wing Attack, Mist, Water Pulse, Payback, Brine, Fling, Stockpile, Swallow, Spit Up, Roost

Young male Pelipper have the task of gathering food while the others guard the nest. With their impressively roomy beaks, they can easily carry enough food for everyone.

EVOLUTION

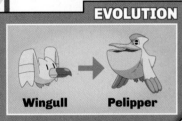

Wingull → Pelipper

PERSIAN (Alola Form)

Classy Cat Pokémon

How to Say It: PER-zhun

Type: Dark

Imperial Height: 3'07"

Metric Height: 1.1 m

Imperial Weight: 72.8 lbs.

Metric Weight: 33.0 kg

Possible Moves: Swift, Quash, Play Rough, Switcheroo, Scratch, Growl, Bite, Fake Out, Fury Swipes, Screech, Feint Attack, Taunt, Power Gem, Slash, Nasty Plot, Assurance, Captivate, Night Slash, Feint, Dark Pulse

Trainers in Alola adore Persian for its coat, which is very smooth and has a velvety texture. This Pokémon has developed a haughty attitude and prefers to fight dirty when it gets into battle.

EVOLUTION

Meowth → Persian

PETILIL

Bulb Pokémon

How to Say It: PEH-tuh-LIL

Type: Grass

Imperial Height: 1'08"

Metric Height: 0.5 m

Imperial Weight: 14.6 lbs.

Metric Weight: 6.6 kg

Possible Moves: Absorb, Growth, Leech Seed, Sleep Powder, Mega Drain, Synthesis, Magical Leaf, Stun Spore, Giga Drain, Aromatherapy, Helping Hand, Energy Ball, Entrainment, Sunny Day, After You, Leaf Storm

Petilil benefits from regular pruning. The leaves that sprout from its head can be brewed into a tea that perks up a weary mind—that is, if you're hardy enough to drink the incredibly bitter concoction!

EVOLUTION

Petilil → Lilligant

PHANTUMP

Stump Pokémon

How to Say It: FAN-tump

Type: Ghost-Grass

Imperial Height: 1'04"

Metric Height: 0.4 m

Imperial Weight: 15.4 lbs.

Metric Weight: 7.0 kg

Possible Moves: Tackle, Confuse Ray, Astonish, Growth, Ingrain, Feint Attack, Leech Seed, Curse, Will-O-Wisp, Forest's Curse, Destiny Bond, Phantom Force, Wood Hammer, Horn Leech

The eerie cry of a Phantump is a reminder of its origin—an old tree stump inhabited by the spirit of a lost child. The leaves on its head are said to possess medicinal qualities.

EVOLUTION

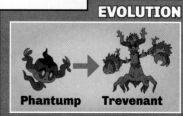

Phantump → Trevenant

PHEROMOSA

Lissome Pokémon

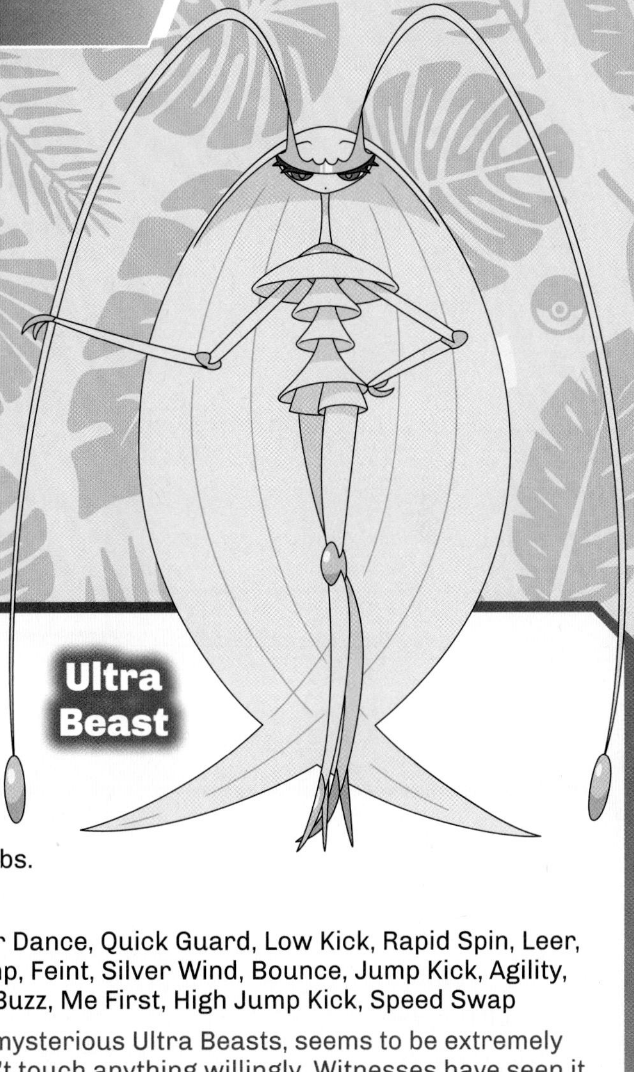

Ultra Beast

How to Say It: fair-uh-MO-suh

Type: Bug-Fighting

Imperial Height: 5'11"

Metric Height: 1.8 m

Imperial Weight: 55.1 lbs.

Metric Weight: 25.0 kg

Possible Moves: Quiver Dance, Quick Guard, Low Kick, Rapid Spin, Leer, Double Kick, Swift, Stomp, Feint, Silver Wind, Bounce, Jump Kick, Agility, Triple Kick, Lunge, Bug Buzz, Me First, High Jump Kick, Speed Swap

Pheromosa, one of the mysterious Ultra Beasts, seems to be extremely wary of germs and won't touch anything willingly. Witnesses have seen it charging through the region at amazing speeds.

EVOLUTION
Does not evolve.

PICHU

Tiny Mouse Pokémon

How to Say It: PEE-choo

Type: Electric

Imperial Height: 1'00"

Metric Height: 0.3 m

Imperial Weight: 4.4 lbs.

Metric Weight: 2.0 kg

Possible Moves: Thunder Shock, Charm, Tail Whip, Sweet Kiss, Nasty Plot, Thunder Wave

Pichu is so adorable, but that doesn't mean it's harmless! Its Trainer has to watch out, because this little Pokémon isn't very good at controlling its own electricity and sometimes shocks itself and others.

EVOLUTION

Pichu   Pikachu   Raichu

PIKACHU

Mouse Pokémon

How to Say It: PEE-ka-choo

Type: Electric

Imperial Height: 1'04"

Metric Height: 0.4 m

Imperial Weight: 13.2 lbs.

Metric Weight: 6.0 kg

Possible Moves: Tail Whip, Thunder Shock, Growl, Play Nice, Quick Attack, Electro Ball, Thunder Wave, Double Team, Spark, Nuzzle, Discharge, Slam, Thunderbolt, Feint, Agility, Wild Charge, Light Screen, Thunder

Pikachu naturally stores up electricity in its body, and it needs to discharge that energy on a regular basis to maintain good health. To take advantage of this, some have suggested creating a Pikachu-fueled power plant.

EVOLUTION

Pichu   Pikachu   Raichu

PIKIPEK

Woodpecker Pokémon

How to Say It: PICK-kee-peck

Type: Normal-Flying

Imperial Height: 1'00"

Metric Height: 0.3 m

Imperial Weight: 2.6 lbs.

Metric Weight: 1.2 kg

Possible Moves: Peck, Growl, Echoed Voice, Rock Smash, Supersonic, Pluck, Roost, Fury Attack, Screech, Drill Peck, Bullet Seed, Feather Dance, Hyper Voice

Pikipek can drill into the side of a tree at the rate of sixteen pecks per second! It uses the resulting hole as a place to nest and to store berries—both for food and for ammunition.

EVOLUTION

Pikipek → Trumbeak → Toucannon

PINSIR

Stag Beetle Pokémon

How to Say It: PIN-sir

Type: Bug

Imperial Height: 4'11"

Metric Height: 1.5 m

Imperial Weight: 121.3 lbs.

Metric Weight: 55.0 kg

Possible Moves: Vice Grip, Focus Energy, Bind, Seismic Toss, Harden, Revenge, Vital Throw, Double Hit, Brick Break, X-Scissor, Submission, Storm Throw, Thrash, Swords Dance, Superpower, Guillotine

Though Pinsir is incredibly tough, it can't cope with cold weather, so it's right at home in Alola—though it does find itself competing with the native Vikavolt. Its horns can lift a much larger foe or topple a tree.

EVOLUTION
Does not evolve.

POLITOED

Frog Pokémon

How to Say It:
PAUL-lee-TOED

Type: Water

Imperial Height: 3'07"

Metric Height: 1.1 m

Imperial Weight: 74.7 lbs.

Metric Weight: 33.9 kg

Possible Moves: Bubble Beam, Hypnosis, Double Slap, Perish Song, Swagger, Bounce, Hyper Voice

When several Politoed gather together to sing under the moon, the angry quality of their cries makes it sound like they're having a heated argument. Poliwag and Poliwhirl regard this Pokémon as a leader.

EVOLUTION

Poliwag

⬇

Poliwhirl

⬇

Politoed

POLIWAG

Tadpole Pokémon

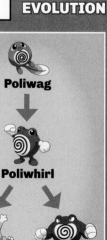

How to Say It: PAUL-lee-wag

Type: Water

Imperial Height: 2'00"

Metric Height: 0.6 m

Imperial Weight: 27.3 lbs.

Metric Weight: 12.4 kg

Possible Moves: Water Sport, Water Gun, Hypnosis, Bubble, Double Slap, Rain Dance, Body Slam, Bubble Beam, Mud Shot, Belly Drum, Wake-Up Slap, Hydro Pump, Mud Bomb

Poliwag's skin is so thin that you can see right through it to the Pokémon's spiral-shaped insides. It's not very skilled at walking on land, but a Trainer can help it get better.

EVOLUTION

Poliwag

⬇

Poliwhirl

⬇

Politoed OR Poliwrath

POLIWHIRL

Tadpole Pokémon

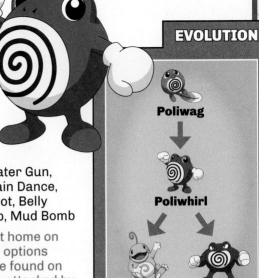

How to Say It: PAUL-lee-wirl

Type: Water

Imperial Height: 3'03"

Metric Height: 1.0 m

Imperial Weight: 44.1 lbs.

Metric Weight: 20.0 kg

Possible Moves: Water Sport, Water Gun, Hypnosis, Bubble, Double Slap, Rain Dance, Body Slam, Bubble Beam, Mud Shot, Belly Drum, Wake-Up Slap, Hydro Pump, Mud Bomb

Poliwhirl is amphibious, equally at home on land or in the water. It weighs the options carefully—there's more food to be found on land, but it's also more likely to be attacked by dangerous Pokémon.

EVOLUTION

Poliwag
↓
Poliwhirl
↓ ↓
Politoed OR Poliwrath

POLIWRATH

Tadpole Pokémon

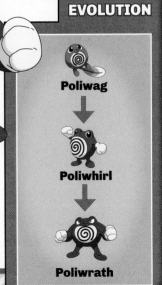

How to Say It: PAUL-lee-rath

Type: Water-Fighting

Imperial Height: 4'03"

Metric Height: 1.3 m

Imperial Weight: 119.0 lbs.

Metric Weight: 54.0 kg

Possible Moves: Submission, Circle Throw, Bubble Beam, Hypnosis, Double Slap, Dynamic Punch, Mind Reader

Kids in Alola often learn to swim by watching local Poliwrath cut through the waves with a powerful breaststroke. This Pokémon's body is dense with muscles, so it has to swim instead of float.

EVOLUTION

Poliwag
↓
Poliwhirl
↓
Poliwrath

POPPLIO

Sea Lion Pokémon

How to Say It:
POP-lee-oh

Type: Water

Imperial Height: 1'04"

Metric Height: 0.4 m

Imperial Weight: 16.5 lbs.

Metric Weight: 7.5 kg

Possible Moves: Pound, Water Gun, Growl, Disarming Voice, Baby-Doll Eyes, Aqua Jet, Encore, Bubble Beam, Sing, Double Slap, Hyper Voice, Moonblast, Captivate, Hydro Pump, Misty Terrain

Popplio uses the water balloons it blows from its nose as a weapon in battle. It's a hard worker and puts in lots of practice creating and controlling these balloons.

EVOLUTION

Popplio → Brionne → Primarina

PORYGON

Virtual Pokémon

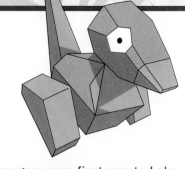

How to Say It: PORE-ee-gon

Type: Normal

Imperial Height: 2'07"

Metric Height: 0.8 m

Imperial Weight: 80.5 lbs.

Metric Weight: 36.5 kg

Possible Moves: Conversion 2, Tackle, Conversion, Sharpen, Psybeam, Agility, Recover, Magnet Rise, Signal Beam, Recycle, Discharge, Lock-On, Tri Attack, Magic Coat, Zap Cannon

Porygon were first created about twenty years ago, and at the time, they were made with cutting-edge technology. By converting itself into data, this Pokémon can travel through cyberspace.

EVOLUTION

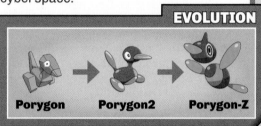

Porygon   Porygon2   Porygon-Z

PORYGON-Z

Virtual Pokémon

How to Say It: PORE-ee-gon ZEE

Type: Normal

Imperial Height: 2'11"

Metric Height: 0.9 m

Imperial Weight: 75.0 lbs.

Metric Weight: 34.0 kg

Possible Moves: Trick Room, Zap Cannon, Magic Coat, Conversion 2, Tackle, Conversion, Nasty Plot, Psybeam, Agility, Recover, Magnet Rise, Signal Beam, Embargo, Discharge, Lock-On, Tri Attack, Zap Cannon, Hyper Beam

Porygon-Z underwent a programming upgrade that was supposed to enable travel between dimensions. Afterward, though, it started to exhibit odd behavior due to an apparent glitch in the new program.

EVOLUTION

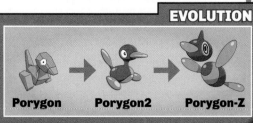

Porygon   Porygon2   Porygon-Z

PORYGON2

Virtual Pokémon

How to Say It: PORE-ee-gon TWO

Type: Normal

Imperial Height: 2'00"

Metric Height: 0.6 m

Imperial Weight: 71.6 lbs.

Metric Weight: 32.5 kg

Possible Moves: Zap Cannon, Magic Coat, Conversion 2, Tackle, Conversion, Defense Curl, Psybeam, Agility, Recover, Magnet Rise, Signal Beam, Recycle, Discharge, Lock-On, Tri Attack, Magic Coat, Zap Cannon, Hyper Beam

Porygon2 came into being when programmers updated the original Porygon with the latest technology. Their goal was to create new developments on other planets, but it hasn't happened yet.

EVOLUTION

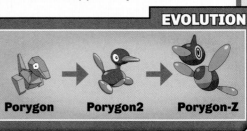

Porygon → Porygon2 → Porygon-Z

PRIMARINA

Soloist Pokémon

How to Say It: PREE-muh-REE-nuh

Type: Water-Fairy

Imperial Height: 5'11"

Metric Height: 1.8 m

Imperial Weight: 97.0 lbs.

Metric Weight: 44.0 kg

Possible Moves: Sparkling Aria, Pound, Water Gun, Growl, Disarming Voice, Baby-Doll Eyes, Aqua Jet, Encore, Bubble Beam, Sing, Double Slap, Hyper Voice, Moonblast, Captivate, Hydro Pump, Misty Terrain

This Pokémon's singing voice is a delicate and powerful weapon, used to attack its foes and to control the water balloons it creates. Groups of Primarina teach these battle songs to the next generation.

EVOLUTION

Popplio → Brionne → Primarina

PRIMEAPE

Pig Monkey Pokémon

How to Say It: PRIME-ape

Type: Fighting

Imperial Height: 3'03"

Metric Height: 1.0 m

Imperial Weight: 70.5 lbs.

Metric Weight: 32.0 kg

Possible Moves: Rage, Final Gambit, Fling, Scratch, Low Kick, Leer, Focus Energy, Fury Swipes, Karate Chop, Pursuit, Seismic Toss, Swagger, Cross Chop, Assurance, Punishment, Thrash, Close Combat, Screech, Stomping Tantrum, Outrage

Primeape's rage can be so intense that the wild emotions coursing through its body put its own health at risk. Even returning it to its Poké Ball might not be enough to calm it down.

EVOLUTION

Mankey   Primeape

PROBOPASS

Compass Pokémon

How to Say It: PRO-bow-pass

Type: Rock-Steel

Imperial Height: 4'07"

Metric Height: 1.4 m

Imperial Weight: 749.6 lbs.

Metric Weight: 340.0 kg

Possible Moves: Tri Attack, Magnetic Flux, Magnet Rise, Gravity, Wide Guard, Tackle, Iron Defense, Block, Magnet Bomb, Thunder Wave, Rest, Spark, Rock Slide, Power Gem, Rock Blast, Discharge, Sandstorm, Earth Power, Stone Edge, Lock-On, Zap Cannon

Probopass sends forth its three small Mini-Noses in strategic maneuvers to outflank an opponent in battle. The magnetic field that surrounds this Pokémon can disrupt or disable electrical devices in the area.

EVOLUTION

Nosepass   Probopass

PSYDUCK

Duck Pokémon

How to Say It: SY-duck

Type: Water

Imperial Height: 2'07"

Metric Height: 0.8 m

Imperial Weight: 43.2 lbs.

Metric Weight: 19.6 kg

Possible Moves: Water Sport, Scratch, Tail Whip, Water Gun, Confusion, Fury Swipes, Water Pulse, Disable, Screech, Zen Headbutt, Aqua Tail, Soak, Psych Up, Amnesia, Hydro Pump, Wonder Room

Poor Psyduck suffers from terrible headaches, which somehow enhance its psychic powers—but it's often too miserable to control those powers. The pain can be intense enough to make it cry.

EVOLUTION

Psyduck   Golduck

PYUKUMUKU

Sea Cucumber Pokémon

How to Say It:
PYOO-koo-MOO-koo

Type: Water

Imperial Height: 1'00"

Metric Height: 0.3 m

Imperial Weight: 2.6 lbs.

Metric Weight: 1.2 kg

Possible Moves: Baton Pass, Water Sport, Mud Sport, Harden, Bide, Helping Hand, Taunt, Safeguard, Counter, Purify, Curse, Gastro Acid, Pain Split, Recover, Soak, Toxic, Memento

Pyukumuku has a remarkable and revolting weapon in battle: It can spew out its innards to strike at its opponent. It's covered in a sticky slime that beachgoers use to soothe their skin after a sunburn.

EVOLUTION
Does not evolve.

RAICHU (Alola Form)

Mouse Pokémon

How to Say It: RYE-choo

Type: Electric-Psychic

Imperial Height: 2'04"

Metric Height: 0.7 m

Imperial Weight: 46.3 lbs.

Metric Weight: 21.0 kg

Possible Moves: Psychic, Speed Swap, Thunder Shock, Tail Whip, Quick Attack, Thunderbolt

Researchers speculate that Raichu looks different in the Alola region because of what it eats. It can "surf" on its own tail, standing on the flat surface and using psychic power to raise itself off the ground.

EVOLUTION

Pichu   Pikachu   Raichu

RAMPARDOS

Head Butt Pokémon

How to Say It: ram-PAR-dose

Type: Rock

Imperial Height: 5'03"

Metric Height: 1.6 m

Imperial Weight: 226.0 lbs.

Metric Weight: 102.5 kg

Possible Moves: Endeavor, Headbutt, Leer, Focus Energy, Pursuit, Take Down, Scary Face, Assurance, Chip Away, Ancient Power, Zen Headbutt, Screech, Head Smash

A headbutt from Rampardos is powerful enough to knock down a tall building. To adapt to this rough treatment, its skull has grown thick and hard—which unfortunately doesn't leave much room for brains.

EVOLUTION

Cranidos   Rampardos

RATICATE (Alola Form)

Mouse Pokémon

How to Say It: RAT-ih-kate

Type: Dark-Normal

Imperial Height: 2'04"

Metric Height: 0.7 m

Imperial Weight: 56.2 lbs.

Metric Weight: 25.5 kg

Possible Moves: Scary Face, Swords Dance, Tackle, Tail Whip, Focus Energy, Quick Attack, Bite, Pursuit, Hyper Fang, Assurance, Crunch, Sucker Punch, Super Fang, Double-Edge, Endeavor

Each Raticate leads a group of Rattata, and the groups regularly scuffle over food. This Pokémon is rather picky about what it eats, so a restaurant where a Raticate lives is likely to be a good one.

EVOLUTION

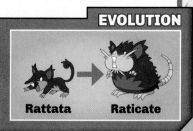

Rattata   Raticate

RATTATA (Alola Form)

Mouse Pokémon

How to Say It: RA-TAT-ta

Type: Dark-Normal

Imperial Height: 1'00"

Metric Height: 0.3 m

Imperial Weight: 8.4 lbs.

Metric Weight: 3.8 kg

Possible Moves: Tackle, Tail Whip, Quick Attack, Focus Energy, Bite, Pursuit, Hyper Fang, Assurance, Crunch, Sucker Punch, Super Fang, Double-Edge, Endeavor

Rattata sleep during the day and spend their nights searching for the best food to bring back to the Raticate who leads them. They use their strong teeth to gnaw their way into people's kitchens.

EVOLUTION

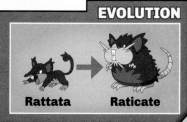

Rattata   Raticate

RELICANTH

Longevity Pokémon

How to Say It:
REL-uh-canth

Type: Water-Rock

Imperial Height: 3'03"

Metric Height: 1.0 m

Imperial Weight: 51.6 lbs.

Metric Weight: 23.4 kg

Possible Moves: Flail, Head Smash, Tackle, Harden, Mud Sport, Water Gun, Rock Tomb, Ancient Power, Dive, Take Down, Yawn, Rest, Hydro Pump, Double-Edge

Relicanth today look much the same as they did 100 million years ago. The abundant fat within their bodies helps them survive the pressure and cold of their deep-sea home.

EVOLUTION
Does not evolve.

RIBOMBEE

Bee Fly Pokémon

How to Say It:
rih-BOMB-bee

Type: Bug-Fairy

Imperial Height: 0'08"

Metric Height: 0.2 m

Imperial Weight: 1.1 lbs.

Metric Weight: 0.5 kg

Possible Moves: Pollen Puff, Absorb, Fairy Wind, Stun Spore, Struggle Bug, Fairy Wind, Silver Wind, Draining Kiss, Sweet Scent, Bug Buzz, Dazzling Gleam, Aromatherapy, Quiver Dance

Ribombee gathers up pollen and forms it into a variety of puffs with different effects. Some enhance battle skills and can be used as supplements, while others deliver excellent nutrition.

EVOLUTION

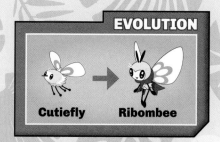

Cutiefly → Ribombee

RIOLU

Emanation Pokémon

How to Say It: ree-OH-loo

Type: Fighting

Imperial Height: 2'04"

Metric Height: 0.7 m

Imperial Weight: 44.5 lbs.

Metric Weight: 20.2 kg

Possible Moves: Foresight, Quick Attack, Endure, Counter, Feint, Force Palm, Copycat, Screech, Reversal, Nasty Plot, Final Gambit

Riolu has a reputation as a hard worker with great stamina. It can sense the auras of others, whether people or Pokémon, and uses this sense to determine how they're doing physically and emotionally.

EVOLUTION

Riolu → Lucario

ROCKRUFF

Puppy Pokémon

How to Say It: ROCK-ruff

Type: Rock

Imperial Height: 1'08"

Metric Height: 0.5 m

Imperial Weight: 20.3 lbs.

Metric Weight: 9.2 kg

Possible Moves: Tackle, Leer, Sand Attack, Bite, Howl, Rock Throw, Odor Sleuth, Rock Tomb, Roar, Stealth Rock, Rock Slide, Scary Face, Crunch, Rock Climb, Stone Edge

Rockruff has a long history of living in harmony with people. This friendly Pokémon is often recommended for Trainers just starting their journey, although it tends to develop a bit of a wild side as it grows.

EVOLUTION

Rockruff → Lycanroc Midday Form

Rockruff → Lycanroc Midnight Form

ROGGENROLA

Mantle Pokémon

How to Say It: rah-gen-ROH-lah

Type: Rock

Imperial Height: 1'04"

Metric Height: 0.4 m

Imperial Weight: 39.7 lbs.

Metric Weight: 18.0 kg

Possible Moves: Tackle, Harden, Sand Attack, Headbutt, Rock Blast, Mud-Slap, Iron Defense, Smack Down, Rock Slide, Stealth Rock, Sandstorm, Stone Edge, Explosion

The cavity that takes up much of Roggenrola's body is an ear, which allows it to track sounds through the darkness of its underground home. These Pokémon compete with Carbink and Geodude to see who has the hardest surface.

EVOLUTION

Roggenrola → Boldore → Gigalith

ROWLET

Grass Quill Pokémon

How to Say It: ROW*-let (*Rhymes with NOW)

Type: Grass-Flying

Imperial Height: 1'00"

Metric Height: 0.3 m

Imperial Weight: 3.3 lbs.

Metric Weight: 1.5 kg

Possible Moves: Tackle, Leafage, Growl, Peck, Astonish, Razor Leaf, Foresight, Pluck, Synthesis, Fury Attack, Sucker Punch, Leaf Blade, Feather Dance, Brave Bird, Nasty Plot

During the day, Rowlet rests and generates energy via photosynthesis. In the night, it flies silently to sneak up on foes and launch a flurry of kicking attacks.

EVOLUTION

Rowlet   Dartrix   Decidueye

RUFFLET

Eaglet Pokémon

How to Say It: RUF-lit

Type: Normal-Flying

Imperial Height: 1'08"

Metric Height: 0.5 m

Imperial Weight: 23.1 lbs.

Metric Weight: 10.5 kg

Possible Moves: Peck, Leer, Fury Attack, Wing Attack, Hone Claws, Scary Face, Aerial Ace, Slash, Defog, Tailwind, Air Slash, Crush Claw, Sky Drop, Whirlwind, Brave Bird, Thrash

Rufflet hasn't yet learned to control its aggressive impulses, and it will pick a fight with just about any opponent. Every defeat makes it stronger, which reinforces its reckless behavior.

EVOLUTION

Rufflet   Braviary

SABLEYE

Darkness Pokémon

How to Say It: SAY-bull-eye

Type: Dark-Ghost

Imperial Height: 1'08"

Metric Height: 0.5 m

Imperial Weight: 24.3 lbs.

Metric Weight: 11.0 kg

Possible Moves: Leer, Scratch, Foresight, Night Shade, Astonish, Fury Swipes, Detect, Shadow Sneak, Feint Attack, Fake Out, Punishment, Knock Off, Shadow Claw, Confuse Ray, Zen Headbutt, Power Gem, Shadow Ball, Foul Play, Quash, Mean Look

Sableye can often be found pursuing Carbink to satisfy their love of shiny gemstones. Stories say this gem-eyed Pokémon can make off with your spirit, so many people avoid them.

EVOLUTION
Does not evolve.

SALAMENCE

Dragon Pokémon

How to Say It: SAL-uh-mence

Type: Dragon-Flying

Imperial Height: 4'11"

Metric Height: 1.5 m

Imperial Weight: 226.2 lbs.

Metric Weight: 102.6 kg

Possible Moves: Fly, Protect, Dragon Tail, Fire Fang, Thunder Fang, Rage, Ember, Leer, Bite, Dragon Breath, Headbutt, Focus Energy, Crunch, Dragon Claw, Zen Headbutt, Scary Face, Flamethrower, Double-Edge

In its delight at finally being able to fly, Salamence sometimes gets a little rowdy. Its fiery celebration can be hazardous to nearby fields and property. It's also inclined to destructive fits of temper.

EVOLUTION

Bagon → Shelgon → Salamence

SALANDIT

Toxic Lizard Pokémon

How to Say It: suh-LAN-dit

Type: Poison-Fire

Imperial Height: 2'00"

Metric Height: 0.6 m

Imperial Weight: 10.6 lbs.

Metric Weight: 4.8 kg

Possible Moves: Scratch, Poison Gas, Ember, Sweet Scent, Dragon Rage, Smog, Double Slap, Flame Burst, Toxic, Nasty Plot, Venoshock, Flamethrower, Venom Drench, Dragon Pulse

Salandit gives off a toxic gas that causes dizziness and confusion when inhaled. It uses this gas to distract opponents before attacking. These Pokémon can often be found living on the slopes of volcanoes.

EVOLUTION

Salandit → Salazzle

SALAZZLE

Toxic Lizard Pokémon

How to Say It: suh-LAZ-zuhl

Type: Poison-Fire

Imperial Height: 3'11"

Metric Height: 1.2 m

Imperial Weight: 48.9 lbs.

Metric Weight: 22.2 kg

Possible Moves: Captivate, Disable, Encore, Torment, Swagger, Pound, Poison Gas, Ember, Sweet Scent, Dragon Rage, Smog, Double Slap, Flame Burst, Toxic, Nasty Plot, Venoshock, Flamethrower, Venom Drench, Dragon Pulse

Apparently, all Salazzle are female. They tend to attract several male Salandit and live together in a group. The poisonous gas they give off contains powerful pheromones and is sometimes used as a perfume ingredient.

EVOLUTION

Salandit → Salazzle

SANDILE

Desert Croc Pokémon

How to Say It: SAN-dyle

Type: Ground-Dark

Imperial Height: 2'04"

Metric Height: 0.7 m

Imperial Weight: 33.5 lbs.

Metric Weight: 15.2 kg

Possible Moves: Leer, Rage, Bite, Sand Attack, Torment, Sand Tomb, Assurance, Mud-Slap, Embargo, Swagger, Crunch, Dig, Scary Face, Foul Play, Sandstorm, Earthquake, Thrash

Keep a sharp eye out if you're walking through the desert. Sandile like to bury themselves in the sand, where they stay hidden and protected from the sun—and if you step on them, you might get chomped!

EVOLUTION

Sandile   **Krokorok**   **Krookodile**

SANDSHREW (Alola Form)

Mouse Pokémon

How to Say It: SAND-shroo

Type: Ice-Steel

Imperial Height: 2'04"

Metric Height: 0.7 m

Imperial Weight: 88.2 lbs.

Metric Weight: 40.0 kg

Possible Moves: Scratch, Defense Curl, Bide, Powder Snow, Ice Ball, Rapid Spin, Fury Cutter, Metal Claw, Swift, Fury Swipes, Iron Defense, Slash, Iron Head, Gyro Ball, Swords Dance, Hail, Blizzard

Sandshrew lives high in the snowy mountains of Alola, where it has developed a shell of thick steel. It's very good at sliding across the ice—whether it does so under its own power or as part of a Sandshrew-sliding contest!

EVOLUTION

Sandshrew   **Sandslash**

SANDSLASH (Alola Form)

Mouse Pokémon

How to Say It: SAND-slash

Type: Ice-Steel

Imperial Height: 3'11"

Metric Height: 1.2 m

Imperial Weight: 121.3 lbs.

Metric Weight: 55.0 kg

Possible Moves: Icicle Spear, Metal Burst, Icicle Crash, Slash, Defense Curl, Ice Ball, Metal Claw

Sandslash is covered in spikes of tough steel, and in the cold mountains where it lives, each spike develops a thick coating of ice. A plume of snow flies up behind it as it dashes across the snowfield.

EVOLUTION

Sandshrew → **Sandslash**

SANDYGAST

Sand Heap Pokémon

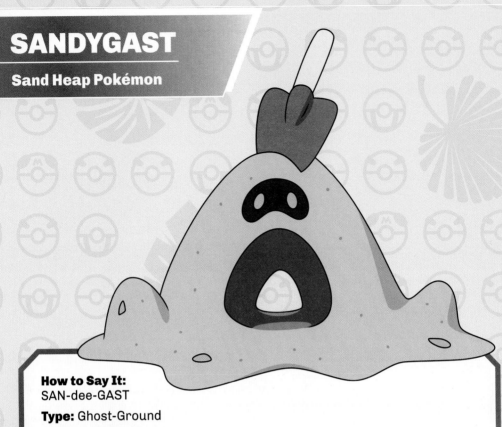

How to Say It:
SAN-dee-GAST

Type: Ghost-Ground

Imperial Height: 1'08"

Metric Height: 0.5 m

Imperial Weight: 154.3 lbs.

Metric Weight: 70.0 kg

Possible Moves: Harden, Absorb, Astonish, Sand Attack, Sand Tomb, Mega Drain, Bulldoze, Hypnosis, Iron Defense, Giga Drain, Shadow Ball, Earth Power, Shore Up, Sandstorm

A child created a mound of sand while playing on the beach, and it became a Sandygast. Putting your hand in its mouth is a sure way to fall prey to its mind control.

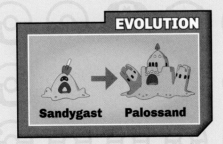

EVOLUTION

Sandygast → Palossand

SCIZOR

Pincer Pokémon

How to Say It: SIH-zor

Type: Bug-Steel

Imperial Height: 5'11"

Metric Height: 1.8 m

Imperial Weight: 260.1 lbs.

Metric Weight: 118.0 kg

Possible Moves: Bullet Punch, Quick Attack, Leer, Focus Energy, Pursuit, False Swipe, Agility, Metal Wing, Fury Cutter, Slash, Razor Wind, Iron Defense, X-Scissor, Night Slash, Double Hit, Iron Head, Swords Dance, Feint

When the hot sun beats down, or when a battle gets really fired up, Scizor can release heat through its wings to keep its metal body from melting. Its steel-hard pincers deliver merciless blows.

EVOLUTION

Scyther → Scizor

SCYTHER

Mantis Pokémon

How to Say It: SY-thur

Type: Bug-Flying

Imperial Height: 4'11"

Metric Height: 1.5 m

Imperial Weight: 123.5 lbs.

Metric Weight: 56.0 kg

Possible Moves: Vacuum Wave, Quick Attack, Leer, Focus Energy, Pursuit, False Swipe, Agility, Wing Attack, Fury Cutter, Slash, Razor Wind, Double Team, X-Scissor, Night Slash, Double Hit, Air Slash, Swords Dance, Feint

Scyther's impressive speed in battle leaves its opponents' heads spinning, which gives it an opening to slash in with its sharp scythes. Young Scyther live in the mountains, where they form groups to train these skills.

EVOLUTION

Scyther → Scizor

SEAKING

Goldfish Pokémon

How to Say It: SEE-king

Type: Water

Imperial Height: 4'03"

Metric Height: 1.3 m

Imperial Weight: 86.0 lbs.

Metric Weight: 39.0 kg

Possible Moves: Megahorn, Poison Jab, Peck, Tail Whip, Water Sport, Supersonic, Horn Attack, Flail, Water Pulse, Aqua Ring, Fury Attack, Agility, Waterfall, Horn Drill, Soak

When autumn arrives, Seaking turns a deep red, just like the leaves on the trees. Fans of this Pokémon tend to argue about which of its features is more admirable: the fins or the horn.

EVOLUTION

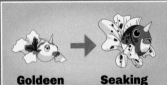

Goldeen → Seaking

SHARPEDO

Brutal Pokémon

How to Say It: shar-PEE-do

Type: Water-Dark

Imperial Height: 5'11"

Metric Height: 1.8 m

Imperial Weight: 195.8 lbs.

Metric Weight: 88.8 kg

Possible Moves: Slash, Night Slash, Feint, Leer, Bite, Rage, Focus Energy, Aqua Jet, Assurance, Screech, Swagger, Ice Fang, Scary Face, Poison Fang, Crunch, Agility, Skull Bash, Taunt

Sharpedo can shoot forward at 75 mph when chasing an enemy. This bully of the sea has teeth that are strong enough to crush iron, and the fin on its back is prized by fishermen.

EVOLUTION

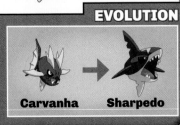

Carvanha → Sharpedo

SHELGON

Endurance Pokémon

How to Say It: SHELL-gon

Type: Dragon

Imperial Height: 3'07"

Metric Height: 1.1 m

Imperial Weight: 243.6 lbs.

Metric Weight: 110.5 kg

Possible Moves: Protect, Rage, Ember, Leer, Bite, Dragon Breath, Headbutt, Focus Energy, Crunch, Dragon Claw, Zen Headbutt, Scary Face, Flamethrower, Double-Edge

From the outside, Shelgon appears completely motionless as it awaits Evolution—but within its shell, it's undergoing rapid changes on a cellular level. During this period, it hides in a cave and consumes no food or water.

EVOLUTION

Bagon → Shelgon → Salamence

SHELLDER

Bivalve Pokémon

How to Say It: SHELL-der

Type: Water

Imperial Height: 1'00"

Metric Height: 0.3 m

Imperial Weight: 8.8 lbs.

Metric Weight: 4.0 kg

Possible Moves: Tackle, Water Gun, Withdraw, Supersonic, Icicle Spear, Protect, Leer, Clamp, Ice Shard, Razor Shell, Aurora Beam, Whirlpool, Brine, Iron Defense, Ice Beam, Shell Smash, Hydro Pump

Shellder shells are so tough and sturdy that they've been used to make shields in the past. If the Pokémon would just pull its tongue in, nothing could ever get to it.

EVOLUTION

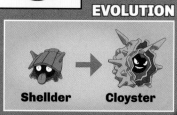

Shellder → Cloyster

SHELLOS (EAST SEA)

Sea Slug Pokémon

How to Say It: SHELL-loss

Type: Water

Imperial Height: 1'00"

Metric Height: 0.3 m

Imperial Weight: 13.9 lbs.

Metric Weight: 6.3 kg

Possible Moves: Mud-Slap, Mud Sport, Harden, Water Pulse, Mud Bomb, Hidden Power, Rain Dance, Body Slam, Muddy Water, Recover

East Sea Shellos are bright blue, reflecting the color of their ocean home. Although the two variants of Shellos look quite different from each other, they have the same battle skills and behaviors.

EVOLUTION

 →

Shellos (East Sea) Gastrodon (East Sea)

SHELLOS (WEST SEA)

Sea Slug Pokémon

How to Say It: SHELL-loss

Type: Water

Imperial Height: 1'00"

Metric Height: 0.3 m

Imperial Weight: 13.9 lbs.

Metric Weight: 6.3 kg

Possible Moves: Mud-Slap, Mud Sport, Harden, Water Pulse, Mud Bomb, Hidden Power, Rain Dance, Body Slam, Muddy Water, Recover

The seashore-dwelling Shellos have varied coloration depending on where they live and what they eat. West Sea Shellos are bright pink.

EVOLUTION

Shellos (West Sea) Gastrodon (West Sea)

SHIELDON

Shield Pokémon

How to Say It:
SHEEL-don

Type: Rock-Steel

Imperial Height: 1'08"

Metric Height: 0.5 m

Imperial Weight: 125.7 lbs.

Metric Weight: 57.0 kg

Possible Moves: Tackle, Protect, Taunt, Metal Sound, Take Down, Iron Defense, Swagger, Ancient Power, Endure, Metal Burst, Iron Head, Heavy Slam

In its own time, this ancient Pokémon lived in the jungle. Many Shieldon fossils have been found, and the heavy armor that protected this Pokémon's face is generally well preserved.

EVOLUTION

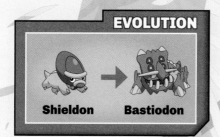

Shieldon → Bastiodon

SHIINOTIC

Illuminating Pokémon

How to Say It: shee-NAH-tick

Type: Grass-Fairy

Imperial Height: 3'03"

Metric Height: 1.0 m

Imperial Weight: 25.4 lbs.

Metric Weight: 11.5 kg

Possible Moves: Absorb, Astonish, Ingrain, Flash, Moonlight, Mega Drain, Sleep Powder, Confuse Ray, Giga Drain, Strength Sap, Spore, Moonblast, Dream Eater, Spotlight

It's a bad idea to wander in Shiinotic's forest home at night. The strange, flickering lights given off by this Pokémon's spores can confuse travelers and cause them to lose their way.

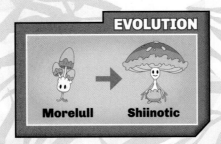

EVOLUTION

Morelull → Shiinotic

SILVALLY

Synthetic Pokémon

How to Say It: sill-VAL-lie

Type: Normal

Imperial Height: 7'07"

Metric Height: 2.3 m

Imperial Weight: 221.6 lbs.

Metric Weight: 100.5 kg

Legendary Pokémon

Possible Moves: Multi-Attack, Heal Block, Imprison, Iron Head, Poison Fang, Fire Fang, Ice Fang, Thunder Fang, Tackle, Rage, Pursuit, Bite, Aerial Ace, Crush Claw, Scary Face, X-Scissor, Take Down, Metal Sound, Crunch, Double Hit, Air Slash, Punishment, Razor Wind, Tri Attack, Double-Edge, Parting Shot

Learning to trust its Trainer caused this Pokémon to evolve and discard the mask that kept its power tightly controlled. Silvally can change its type in battle, making it a formidable opponent.

EVOLUTION

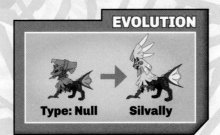

Type: Null → Silvally

SKARMORY

Armor Bird Pokémon

EVOLUTION
Does not evolve.

How to Say It: SKAR-more-ree

Type: Steel-Flying

Imperial Height: 5'07"

Metric Height: 1.7 m

Imperial Weight: 111.3 lbs.

Metric Weight: 50.5 kg

Possible Moves: Leer, Peck, Sand Attack, Metal Claw, Air Cutter, Fury Attack, Feint, Swift, Spikes, Agility, Steel Wing, Slash, Metal Sound, Air Slash, Autotomize, Night Slash

Skarmory sheds its sharp-edged feathers as it grows, and warriors of old would collect them for use as weapons. When it rains, Skarmory stays in its nest so its metal doesn't rust.

SLIGGOO

Soft Tissue Pokémon

How to Say It: SLIH-goo

Type: Dragon

Imperial Height: 2'07"

Metric Height: 0.8 m

Imperial Weight: 38.6 lbs.

Metric Weight: 17.5 kg

Possible Moves: Tackle, Bubble, Absorb, Protect, Bide, Dragon Breath, Rain Dance, Flail, Body Slam, Muddy Water, Dragon Pulse

Sliggoo doesn't have teeth, so it has to dissolve its food before eating. The mucus it sprays can cause just about anything to melt, given enough time.

EVOLUTION

Goomy → Sliggoo → Goodra

SLOWBRO

Hermit Crab Pokémon

How to Say It: SLOW-bro

Type: Water-Psychic

Imperial Height: 5'03"

Metric Height: 1.6 m

Imperial Weight: 173.1 lbs.

Metric Weight: 78.5 kg

Possible Moves: Withdraw, Heal Pulse, Curse, Yawn, Tackle, Growl, Water Gun, Confusion, Disable, Headbutt, Water Pulse, Zen Headbutt, Slack Off, Amnesia, Psychic, Rain Dance, Psych Up

Thanks to Shellder's poisonous bite, Slowbro has grown even more scatterbrained, content to stare at the sea and let its mind wander. It's occasionally startled into a moment of insight—but that moment passes just as quickly.

EVOLUTION

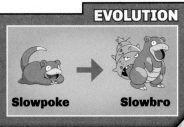

Slowpoke → Slowbro

SLOWKING

Royal Pokémon

How to Say It: SLOW-king

Type: Water-Psychic

Imperial Height: 6'07"

Metric Height: 2.0 m

Imperial Weight: 175.3 lbs.

Metric Weight: 79.5 kg

Possible Moves: Heal Pulse, Power Gem, Hidden Power, Curse, Yawn, Tackle, Growl, Water Gun, Confusion, Disable, Headbutt, Water Pulse, Zen Headbutt, Nasty Plot, Swagger, Psychic, Trump Card, Psych Up

When Slowking was bitten on the head, the poisons that were released interacted with its system in a mysterious way, enhancing its brainpower to the point of genius.

EVOLUTION

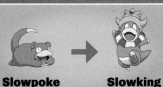

Slowpoke → Slowking

SLOWPOKE

Dopey Pokémon

How to Say It: SLOW-poke
Type: Water-Psychic
Imperial Height: 3'11"
Metric Height: 1.2 m
Imperial Weight: 79.4 lbs.
Metric Weight: 36.0 kg

Possible Moves: Curse, Yawn, Tackle, Growl, Water Gun, Confusion, Disable, Headbutt, Water Pulse, Zen Headbutt, Slack Off, Amnesia, Psychic, Rain Dance, Psych Up, Heal Pulse

If Slowpoke's tail breaks off as it goes about its business, it probably won't even notice, and a new one will grow in quickly. The discarded tail can be dried for use in cooking.

EVOLUTION

Slowpoke → Slowbro
Slowpoke → Slowking

SMEARGLE

Painter Pokémon

How to Say It: SMEAR-gull
Type: Normal
Imperial Height: 3'11"
Metric Height: 1.2 m
Imperial Weight: 127.9 lbs.
Metric Weight: 58.0 kg
Possible Move: Sketch

Smeargle's tail tip produces a fluid that it uses like paint—it literally marks its territory, using many different symbols. Towns with an apparent graffiti problem might just be home to lots of Smeargle.

EVOLUTION
Does not evolve.

SNEASEL

Sharp Claw Pokémon

How to Say It: SNEE-zul

Type: Dark-Ice

Imperial Height: 2'11"

Metric Height: 0.9 m

Imperial Weight: 61.7 lbs.

Metric Weight: 28.0 kg

Possible Moves: Scratch, Leer, Taunt, Quick Attack, Feint Attack, Icy Wind, Fury Swipes, Agility, Metal Claw, Hone Claws, Beat Up, Screech, Slash, Snatch, Punishment, Ice Shard

Sneasel has a reputation as a crafty, vicious egg thief. It lies in wait until a nest is left unguarded, then strikes quickly and stealthily with its sharp claws.

EVOLUTION

Sneasel → Weavile

SNORLAX

Sleeping Pokémon

How to Say It: SNOR-lacks

Type: Normal

Imperial Height: 6'11"

Metric Height: 2.1 m

Imperial Weight: 1,014.1 lbs.

Metric Weight: 460.0 kg

Possible Moves: Tackle, Defense Curl, Amnesia, Lick, Chip Away, Yawn, Body Slam, Rest, Snore, Sleep Talk, Giga Impact, Rollout, Block, Belly Drum, Crunch, Heavy Slam, High Horsepower

The stomach of a Snorlax can handle just about anything—which is fortunate, because its massive body requires nearly 900 pounds of food every day. If it dozes off during a meal, it can keep eating in its sleep.

EVOLUTION

Munchlax → Snorlax

SNORUNT

Snow Hat Pokémon

How to Say It: SNOW-runt

Type: Ice

Imperial Height: 2'04"

Metric Height: 0.7 m

Imperial Weight: 37.0 lbs.

Metric Weight: 16.8 kg

Possible Moves: Powder Snow, Leer, Double Team, Ice Shard, Icy Wind, Bite, Ice Fang, Headbutt, Protect, Frost Breath, Crunch, Blizzard, Hail

If a Snorunt comes to visit, don't shoo it away! According to tradition, having a Snorunt living in your house guarantees prosperity for many years. This Pokémon is quite happy in the bitter cold.

EVOLUTION

Snorunt → Froslass

Snorunt → Glalie

SNUBBULL

Fairy Pokémon

How to Say It: SNUB-bull

Type: Fairy

Imperial Height: 2'00"

Metric Height: 0.6 m

Imperial Weight: 17.2 lbs.

Metric Weight: 7.8 kg

Possible Moves: Ice Fang, Fire Fang, Thunder Fang, Tackle, Scary Face, Tail Whip, Charm, Bite, Lick, Headbutt, Roar, Rage, Play Rough, Payback, Crunch

Snubbull might look scary, but it's a big wimp, often too cowardly or too lazy to pick a fight. It attempts to drive off a would-be opponent with a growl—but many people find this adorable.

EVOLUTION

Snubbull → Granbull

SOLGALEO

Sunne Pokémon

Legendary Pokémon

How to Say It: SOUL-gah-LAY-oh

Type: Psychic-Steel

Imperial Height: 11'02"

Metric Height: 3.4 m

Imperial Weight: 507.1 lbs.

Metric Weight: 230.0 kg

Possible Moves: Sunsteel Strike, Cosmic Power, Wake-Up Slap, Teleport, Metal Claw, Iron Head, Metal Sound, Zen Headbutt, Flash Cannon, Morning Sun, Crunch, Metal Burst, Solar Beam, Noble Roar, Flare Blitz, Wide Guard, Giga Impact

Solgaleo's entire body radiates a bright light that can wipe away the darkness of night. This Legendary Pokémon apparently makes its home in another world, and it returns there when its third eye becomes active.

EVOLUTION

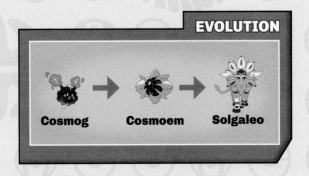

Cosmog → Cosmoem → Solgaleo

SPEAROW

Tiny Bird Pokémon

How to Say It: SPEER-oh

Type: Normal-Flying

Imperial Height: 1'00"

Metric Height: 0.3 m

Imperial Weight: 4.4 lbs.

Metric Weight: 2.0 kg

Possible Moves: Peck, Growl, Leer, Pursuit, Fury Attack, Aerial Ace, Mirror Move, Assurance, Agility, Focus Energy, Roost, Drill Peck

Spearow's wings are too short for effective flying, so they stay on the ground and move about with rapid hops. They drive off so many Bug-types that farmers really like having them around.

EVOLUTION

Spearow → Fearow

SPINARAK

String Spit Pokémon

How to Say It: SPIN-uh-rack

Type: Bug-Poison

Imperial Height: 1'08"

Metric Height: 0.5 m

Imperial Weight: 18.7 lbs.

Metric Weight: 8.5 kg

Possible Moves: Poison Sting, String Shot, Constrict, Absorb, Infestation, Scary Face, Night Shade, Shadow Sneak, Fury Swipes, Sucker Punch, Spider Web, Agility, Pin Missile, Psychic, Poison Jab, Cross Poison, Sticky Web, Toxic Thread

The threads Spinarak uses to spin its web are so sturdy that they're sometimes used to reinforce fishing nets. Rather than go out hunting for food, this patient Pokémon waits for something to blunder into its web.

EVOLUTION

Spinarak → Ariados

SPINDA

Spot Panda Pokémon

How to Say It: SPIN-dah

Type: Normal

Imperial Height: 3'07"

Metric Height: 1.1 m

Imperial Weight: 11.0 lbs.

Metric Weight: 5.0 kg

Possible Moves: Tackle, Copycat, Feint Attack, Psybeam, Hypnosis, Dizzy Punch, Sucker Punch, Teeter Dance, Uproar, Psych Up, Double-Edge, Flail, Thrash

As Spinda staggers and totters about, it has the mistaken impression that it's walking straight. Each Spinda's spot pattern is slightly different, and collectors appreciate the variety.

EVOLUTION
Does not evolve.

STARMIE

Mysterious Pokémon

How to Say It: STAR-mee

Type: Water-Psychic

Imperial Height: 3'07"

Metric Height: 1.1 m

Imperial Weight: 176.4 lbs.

Metric Weight: 80.0 kg

Possible Moves: Hydro Pump, Spotlight, Water Gun, Rapid Spin, Recover, Swift, Confuse Ray

Getting close to a Starmie could give you a headache, possibly because of mysterious signals transmitted by its glowing core. With a shape like a many-pointed star, could this Pokémon have fallen from outer space?

EVOLUTION

Staryu → Starmie

STARYU

Star Shape Pokémon

How to Say It: STAR-you

Type: Water

Imperial Height: 2'07"

Metric Height: 0.8 m

Imperial Weight: 76.1 lbs.

Metric Weight: 34.5 kg

Possible Moves: Tackle, Harden, Water Gun, Rapid Spin, Recover, Psywave, Swift, Bubble Beam, Camouflage, Gyro Ball, Brine, Minimize, Reflect Type, Power Gem, Confuse Ray, Psychic, Light Screen, Cosmic Power, Hydro Pump

A cluster of red lights glowing on the beach at night is probably a Staryu colony. Its red core glows at night, and as long as the core is whole, this Pokémon can regenerate from almost any injury.

EVOLUTION

Staryu → Starmie

STEENEE

Fruit Pokémon

How to Say It: STEE-nee

Type: Grass

Imperial Height: 2'04"

Metric Height: 0.7 m

Imperial Weight: 18.1 lbs.

Metric Weight: 8.2 kg

Possible Moves: Double Slap, Splash, Play Nice, Rapid Spin, Razor Leaf, Sweet Scent, Magical Leaf, Teeter Dance, Stomp, Aromatic Mist, Captivate, Aromatherapy, Leaf Storm

Lively and cheerful, Steenee often attracts a crowd of other Pokémon drawn to its energy and its lovely scent. Its sepals have evolved into a hard shell to protect its head and body from attackers.

EVOLUTION

Bounsweet → Steenee → Tsareena

STOUTLAND

Big-Hearted Pokémon

How to Say It: STOWT-lund

Type: Normal

Imperial Height: 3'11"

Metric Height: 1.2 m

Imperial Weight: 134.5 lbs.

Metric Weight: 61.0 kg

Possible Moves: Ice Fang, Fire Fang, Thunder Fang, Leer, Tackle, Odor Sleuth, Bite, Helping Hand, Take Down, Work Up, Crunch, Roar, Retaliate, Reversal, Last Resort, Giga Impact, Play Rough

Stoutland's bravery and intelligence make it an excellent partner. Many Trainers put their trust in this Pokémon to help rescue explorers stranded in the mountains—or to keep an eye on the kids.

EVOLUTION

Lillipup → Herdier → Stoutland

STUFFUL

Flailing Pokémon

How to Say It: STUFF-fuhl

Type: Normal-Fighting

Imperial Height: 1'08"

Metric Height: 0.5 m

Imperial Weight: 15.0 lbs.

Metric Weight: 6.8 kg

Possible Moves: Tackle, Leer, Bide, Baby-Doll Eyes, Brutal Swing, Flail, Payback, Take Down, Hammer Arm, Thrash, Pain Split, Double-Edge, Superpower

Petting an unfamiliar Stufful is a bad idea, even though it's really cute—it dislikes being touched by anyone it doesn't consider a friend, and responds with a flailing of limbs that can knock over a strong fighter.

EVOLUTION

Stufful → Bewear

SUDOWOODO

Imitation Pokémon

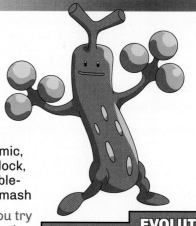

How to Say It: SOO-doe-WOO-doe

Type: Rock

Imperial Height: 3'11"

Metric Height: 1.2 m

Imperial Weight: 83.8 lbs.

Metric Weight: 38.0 kg

Possible Moves: Slam, Wood Hammer, Copycat, Flail, Low Kick, Rock Throw, Mimic, Feint Attack, Tearful Look, Rock Tomb, Block, Rock Slide, Counter, Sucker Punch, Double-Edge, Stone Edge, Hammer Arm, Head Smash

Sudowoodo may look like a tree, but if you try to water it, it will run away! This Pokémon is favored by elderly Trainers and is sometimes sought after by collectors, who prefer Sudowoodo with bigger patches of green.

EVOLUTION

Bonsly → Sudowoodo

SURSKIT

Pond Skater Pokémon

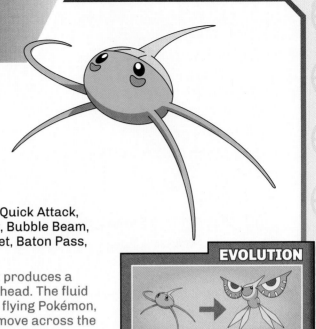

How to Say It: SUR-skit

Type: Bug-Water

Imperial Height: 1'08"

Metric Height: 0.5 m

Imperial Weight: 3.7 lbs.

Metric Weight: 1.7 kg

Possible Moves: Bubble, Quick Attack, Sweet Scent, Water Sport, Bubble Beam, Agility, Mist, Haze, Aqua Jet, Baton Pass, Sticky Web

When threatened, Surskit produces a fluid from the point on its head. The fluid tastes very unpleasant to flying Pokémon, so they stay away. It can move across the water's surface as if it's skating.

EVOLUTION

Surskit → Masquerain

SYLVEON

Intertwining Pokémon

How to Say It: SIL-vee-on

Type: Fairy

Imperial Height: 3'03"

Metric Height: 1.0 m

Imperial Weight: 51.8 lbs.

Metric Weight: 23.5 kg

Possible Moves: Fairy Wind, Disarming Voice, Helping Hand, Tackle, Tail Whip, Sand Attack, Baby-Doll Eyes, Quick Attack, Swift, Draining Kiss, Skill Swap, Misty Terrain, Light Screen, Moonblast, Last Resort, Psych Up

Sylveon projects a calming aura from its feelers, which look like flowing ribbons. It sometimes uses this aura in battle to trick its opponents into dropping their defenses.

EVOLUTION

Eevee → Sylveon

TALONFLAME

Scorching Pokémon

How to Say It: TAL-un-flame

Type: Fire-Flying

Imperial Height: 3'11"

Metric Height: 1.2 m

Imperial Weight: 54.0 lbs.

Metric Weight: 24.5 kg

Possible Moves: Ember, Flare Blitz, Tackle, Growl, Quick Attack, Peck, Agility, Flail, Roost, Razor Wind, Natural Gift, Flame Charge, Acrobatics, Me First, Tailwind, Steel Wing, Brave Bird

Talonflame can swoop at incredible speeds when attacking, which enhances the already impressive power of its kick. Its wings give off showers of embers as it flies.

EVOLUTION

Fletchling → Fletchinder → Talonflame

TAPU BULU

Land Spirit Pokémon

How to Say It: TAH-poo BOO-loo

Type: Grass-Fairy

Imperial Height: 6'03"

Metric Height: 1.9 m

Imperial Weight: 100.3 lbs.

Metric Weight: 45.5 kg

Possible Moves: Grassy Terrain, Wood Hammer, Superpower, Mean Look, Disable, Whirlwind, Withdraw, Leafage, Horn Attack, Giga Drain, Scary Face, Leech Seed, Horn Leech, Rototiller, Nature's Madness, Zen Headbutt, Megahorn, Skull Bash

Tapu Bulu has a reputation for laziness—rather than battling directly, it commands vines to pin down its foes. The plants that grow abundantly in its wake give it energy. It's known as the guardian deity of Ula'ula Island.

Legendary Pokémon

EVOLUTION
Does not evolve.

TAPU FINI

Land Spirit Pokémon

Legendary Pokémon

How to Say It: TAH-poo FEE-nee

Type: Water-Fairy

Imperial Height: 4'03"

Metric Height: 1.3 m

Imperial Weight: 46.7 lbs.

Metric Weight: 21.2 kg

Possible Moves: Misty Terrain, Moonblast, Heal Pulse, Mean Look, Haze, Mist, Withdraw, Water Gun, Water Pulse, Whirlpool, Soak, Refresh, Brine, Defog, Nature's Madness, Muddy Water, Aqua Ring, Hydro Pump

Tapu Fini can control and cleanse water, washing away impurities. When threatened, it summons a dense fog to confuse its enemies. This Pokémon draws energy from ocean currents. It's known as the guardian deity of Poni Island.

EVOLUTION
Does not evolve.

TAPU KOKO

Land Spirit Pokémon

Legendary Pokémon

How to Say It: TAH-poo KO-ko

Type: Electric-Fairy

Imperial Height: 5'11"

Metric Height: 1.8 m

Imperial Weight: 45.2 lbs.

Metric Weight: 20.5 kg

Possible Moves: Electric Terrain, Brave Bird, Power Swap, Mean Look, Quick Attack, False Swipe, Withdraw, Thunder Shock, Spark, Shock Wave, Screech, Charge, Wild Charge, Mirror Move, Nature's Madness, Discharge, Agility, Electro Ball

Somewhat lacking in attention span, Tapu Koko is quick to anger but just as quickly forgets why it's angry. Calling thunderclouds lets it store up lightning as energy. It's known as the guardian deity of Melemele Island.

EVOLUTION
Does not evolve.

TAPU LELE

Land Spirit Pokémon

Legendary Pokémon

How to Say It: TAH-poo LEH-leh

Type: Psychic-Fairy

Imperial Height: 3'11"

Metric Height: 1.2 m

Imperial Weight: 41.0 lbs.

Metric Weight: 18.6 kg

Possible Moves: Psychic Terrain, Aromatic Mist, Aromatherapy, Mean Look, Draining Kiss, Astonish, Withdraw, Confusion, Psywave, Psybeam, Sweet Scent, Skill Swap, Psyshock, Tickle, Nature's Madness, Extrasensory, Flatter, Moonblast

As Tapu Lele flutters through the air, people in search of good health gather up the glowing scales that fall from its body. It draws energy from the scent of flowers. It's known as the guardian deity of Akala Island.

EVOLUTION
Does not evolve.

TAUROS

Wild Bull Pokémon

How to Say It: TORE-ros

Type: Normal

Imperial Height: 4'07"

Metric Height: 1.4 m

Imperial Weight: 194.9 lbs.

Metric Weight: 88.4 kg

Possible Moves: Tackle, Tail Whip, Rage, Horn Attack, Scary Face, Pursuit, Rest, Payback, Work Up, Zen Headbutt, Take Down, Swagger, Thrash, Giga Impact

Although Tauros in other regions are known for their fierce love of battle, the Tauros in Alola are calm enough that many people can ride them without fear. The practice of Tauros riding can apparently be traced to this region.

EVOLUTION
Does not evolve.

TENTACOOL

Jellyfish Pokémon

How to Say It: TEN-ta-cool

Type: Water-Poison

Imperial Height: 2'11"

Metric Height: 0.9 m

Imperial Weight: 100.3 lbs.

Metric Weight: 45.5 kg

Possible Moves: Poison Sting, Supersonic, Constrict, Acid, Toxic Spikes, Water Pulse, Wrap, Acid Spray, Bubble Beam, Barrier, Poison Jab, Brine, Screech, Hex, Sludge Wave, Hydro Pump, Wring Out

If you find a dried-out Tentacool on the beach, you could try soaking it in water to restore it to good health. Watch out, though—its tentacles carry a poison that could send you to the hospital.

EVOLUTION

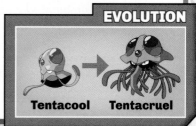

Tentacool   **Tentacruel**

TENTACRUEL

Jellyfish Pokémon

How to Say It: TEN-ta-crool

Type: Water-Poison

Imperial Height: 5'03"

Metric Height: 1.6 m

Imperial Weight: 121.3 lbs.

Metric Weight: 55.0 kg

Possible Moves: Reflect Type, Wring Out, Poison Sting, Supersonic, Constrict, Acid, Toxic Spikes, Water Pulse, Wrap, Acid Spray, Bubble Beam, Barrier, Poison Jab, Brine, Screech, Hex, Sludge Wave, Hydro Pump

Tentacruel starts out with eighty tentacles, all packed with nasty poison. As it grows older, some of its tentacles are damaged or broken off in battle. When many Tentacruel gather, other Pokémon flee the area.

EVOLUTION

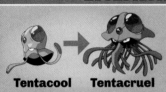

Tentacool → Tentacruel

TIRTOUGA

Prototurtle Pokémon

How to Say It: teer-TOO-gah

Type: Water-Rock

Imperial Height: 2'04"

Metric Height: 0.7 m

Imperial Weight: 36.4 lbs.

Metric Weight: 16.5 kg

Possible Moves: Bide, Withdraw, Water Gun, Rollout, Bite, Protect, Aqua Jet, Ancient Power, Crunch, Wide Guard, Brine, Smack Down, Curse, Shell Smash, Aqua Tail, Rock Slide, Rain Dance, Hydro Pump

Studies of Tirtouga's fossilized skeleton indicate that it could reach depths of half a mile when diving in the warm oceans of its ancient home. It originally lived 100 million years ago.

EVOLUTION

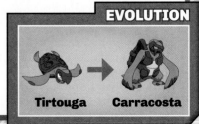

Tirtouga → Carracosta

TOGEDEMARU

Roly-Poly Pokémon

How to Say It:
TOH-geh-deh-MAH-roo

Type: Electric-Steel

Imperial Height: 1'00"

Metric Height: 0.3 m

Imperial Weight: 7.3 lbs.

Metric Weight: 3.3 kg

Possible Moves: Tackle, Thunder Shock, Defense Curl, Rollout, Charge, Spark, Nuzzle, Magnet Rise, Discharge, Zing Zap, Electric Terrain, Wild Charge, Pin Missile, Spiky Shield, Fell Stinger

Its back is covered with long, spiny fur that usually lies flat. Togedemaru can bristle up the fur during battle for use as a weapon or during storms to attract lightning, which it stores as electricity in its body.

EVOLUTION
Does not evolve.

TORKOAL

Coal Pokémon

How to Say It: TOR-coal

Type: Fire

Imperial Height: 1'08"

Metric Height: 0.5 m

Imperial Weight: 177.2 lbs.

Metric Weight: 80.4 kg

Possible Moves: Ember, Smog, Withdraw, Rapid Spin, Fire Spin, Smokescreen, Flame Wheel, Curse, Lava Plume, Body Slam, Protect, Flamethrower, Iron Defense, Amnesia, Flail, Heat Wave, Shell Smash, Inferno

Because wild Torkoal get their energy by burning coal within their shells, they tend to live near large coal deposits in the mountains. A Trainer who has Torkoal as a partner must keep a steady source of fuel on hand.

EVOLUTION
Does not evolve.

TORRACAT

Fire Cat Pokémon

How to Say It: TOR-ruh-cat

Type: Fire

Imperial Height: 2'04"

Metric Height: 0.7 m

Imperial Weight: 55.1 lbs.

Metric Weight: 25.0 kg

Possible Moves: Scratch, Ember, Growl, Lick, Leer, Fire Fang, Roar, Bite, Swagger, Fury Swipes, Thrash, Flamethrower, Scary Face, Flare Blitz, Outrage

Torracat attacks with powerful punches from its front legs, which are strong enough to bend iron. When it spits flames, the fiery bell at its throat starts to ring.

EVOLUTION

Litten → **Torracat** → **Incineroar**

TOUCANNON

Cannon Pokémon

The inside of Toucannon's beak gets very hot during a battle—over two hundred degrees Fahrenheit. The heat fuels its explosive seed-shooting and can also cause serious burns to its opponent.

How to Say It:
too-CAN-nun

Type: Normal-Flying

Imperial Height: 3'07"

Metric Height: 1.1 m

Imperial Weight: 57.3 lbs.

Metric Weight: 26.0 kg

Possible Moves: Beak Blast, Rock Blast, Peck, Growl, Echoed Voice, Rock Smash, Supersonic, Pluck, Roost, Fury Attack, Screech, Drill Peck, Bullet Seed, Feather Dance, Hyper Voice

EVOLUTION

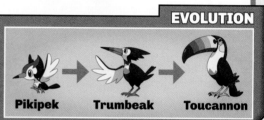

Pikipek → Trumbeak → Toucannon

TOXAPEX

Brutal Star Pokémon

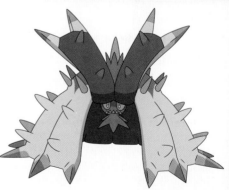

How to Say It: TOX-uh-pex

Type: Poison-Water

Imperial Height: 2'04"

Metric Height: 0.7 m

Imperial Weight: 32.0 lbs.

Metric Weight: 14.5 kg

Possible Moves: Baneful Bunker, Poison Sting, Peck, Bite, Toxic Spikes, Wide Guard, Toxic, Venoshock, Spike Cannon, Recover, Poison Jab, Venom Drench, Pin Missile, Liquidation

It's a good thing Toxapex lives at the bottom of the ocean, because its poison is very dangerous. Those who fall prey to it can expect three very painful days before they recover, and the effects can linger.

EVOLUTION

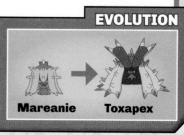

Mareanie → Toxapex

TRAPINCH

Ant Pit Pokémon

How to Say It: TRAP-inch

Type: Ground

Imperial Height: 2'04"

Metric Height: 0.7 m

Imperial Weight: 33.1 lbs.

Metric Weight: 15.0 kg

Possible Moves: Sand Attack, Bite, Feint Attack, Bide, Mud-Slap, Bulldoze, Sand Tomb, Rock Slide, Dig, Crunch, Earth Power, Feint, Earthquake, Sandstorm, Superpower, Hyper Beam, Fissure

Trapinch's huge jaws can easily crush rocks while it's digging through the sand to create its nest. This patient Pokémon waits for something edible to fall into its nest, which looks like a funnel.

EVOLUTION

Trapinch → Vibrava → Flygon

TREVENANT

Elder Tree Pokémon

How to Say It: TREV-uh-nunt

Type: Ghost-Grass

Imperial Height: 4'11"

Metric Height: 1.5 m

Imperial Weight: 156.5 lbs.

Metric Weight: 71.0 kg

Possible Moves: Shadow Claw, Horn Leech, Tackle, Confuse Ray, Astonish, Growth, Ingrain, Feint Attack, Leech Seed, Curse, Will-O-Wisp, Forest's Curse, Destiny Bond, Phantom Force, Wood Hammer

Trevenant serves as a guardian to its forest home and protects the creatures who live there. Anyone who tries to harm the forest will surely face its wrath.

EVOLUTION

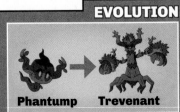

Phantump → Trevenant

TRUBBISH

Trash Bag Pokémon

How to Say It: TRUB-bish

Type: Poison

Imperial Height: 2'00"

Metric Height: 0.6 m

Imperial Weight: 68.3 lbs.

Metric Weight: 31.0 kg

Possible Moves: Pound, Poison Gas, Recycle, Toxic Spikes, Acid Spray, Double Slap, Sludge, Stockpile, Swallow, Take Down, Sludge Bomb, Clear Smog, Toxic, Amnesia, Belch, Gunk Shot, Explosion

When Trubbish encounters tasty trash, it will munch until it's completely full, and the gases it gives off afterward can be toxic. In Alola, Trubbish and Grimer often battle over sources of delicious garbage.

EVOLUTION

Trubbish   Garbodor

TRUMBEAK

Bugle Beak Pokémon

How to Say It: TRUM-beak

Type: Normal-Flying

Imperial Height: 2'00"

Metric Height: 0.6 m

Imperial Weight: 32.6 lbs.

Metric Weight: 14.8 kg

Possible Moves: Rock Blast, Peck, Growl, Echoed Voice, Rock Smash, Supersonic, Pluck, Roost, Fury Attack, Screech, Drill Peck, Bullet Seed, Feather Dance, Hyper Voice

Trumbeak stores berry seeds in its beak to use as ammunition. It attacks opponents with a rapid-fire burst of seeds. Its beak is also very good at making lots of noise!

EVOLUTION

Pikipek   Trumbeak   Toucannon

TSAREENA

Fruit Pokémon

How to Say It: zar-EE-nuh

Type: Grass

Imperial Height: 3'11"

Metric Height: 1.2 m

Imperial Weight: 47.2 lbs.

Metric Weight: 21.4 kg

Possible Moves: Trop Kick, Double Slap, Splash, Swagger, Rapid Spin, Razor Leaf, Sweet Scent, Magical Leaf, Teeter Dance, Stomp, Aromatic Mist, Captivate, Aromatherapy, Leaf Storm, High Jump Kick

Beauty salons sometimes use images of the lovely Tsareena in their advertising. It can be a fierce fighter, using its long legs to deliver skillful kicks as it mocks its defeated opponent.

EVOLUTION

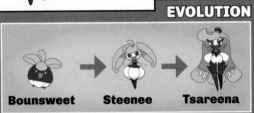

Bounsweet → **Steenee** → **Tsareena**

TURTONATOR

Blast Turtle Pokémon

How to Say It: TURT-nay-ter

Type: Fire-Dragon

Imperial Height: 6'07"

Metric Height: 2.0 m

Imperial Weight: 467.4 lbs.

Metric Weight: 212.0 kg

Possible Moves: Ember, Tackle, Smog, Protect, Incinerate, Flail, Endure, Iron Defense, Flamethrower, Body Slam, Shell Smash, Dragon Pulse, Shell Trap, Overheat, Explosion

Poisonous gases and flames spew from Turtonator's nostrils. Its shell is made of unstable material that might explode upon impact, so opponents are advised to aim for its stomach instead.

EVOLUTION
Does not evolve.

TYPE: NULL

Synthetic Pokémon

Legendary Pokémon

How to Say It:
TYPE NULL

Type: Normal

Imperial Height: 6'03"

Metric Height: 1.9 m

Imperial Weight: 265.7 lbs.

Metric Weight: 120.5 kg

Possible Moves: Tackle, Rage, Pursuit, Imprison, Aerial Ace, Crush Claw, Scary Face, X-Scissor, Take Down, Metal Sound, Iron Head, Double Hit, Air Slash, Punishment, Razor Wind, Tri Attack, Double-Edge, Heal Block

The synthetic Pokémon known as Type: Null wears a heavy mask to keep its power in check. Some fear that without the mask, it would lose control of its powers and go on a destructive rampage.

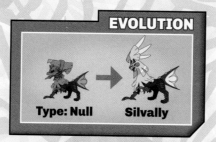

EVOLUTION

Type: Null → Silvally

177

UMBREON

Moonlight Pokémon

How to Say It:
UM-bree-on

Type: Dark

Imperial Height: 3'03"

Metric Height: 1.0 m

Imperial Weight: 59.5 lbs.

Metric Weight: 27.0 kg

Possible Moves: Pursuit, Helping Hand, Tackle, Tail Whip, Sand Attack, Baby-Doll Eyes, Quick Attack, Confuse Ray, Feint Attack, Assurance, Screech, Moonlight, Mean Look, Last Resort, Guard Swap

Umbreon's black fur makes it well suited for battles in the dark. It can rely on this camouflage to keep it hidden until it's ready to strike. When it's angry, its sweat turns toxic.

EVOLUTION

Eevee → Umbreon

VANILLISH

Icy Snow Pokémon

How to Say It: vuh-NIHL-lish

Type: Ice

Imperial Height: 3'07"

Metric Height: 1.1 m

Imperial Weight: 90.4 lbs.

Metric Weight: 41.0 kg

Possible Moves: Icicle Spear, Harden, Astonish, Uproar, Icy Wind, Mist, Avalanche, Taunt, Mirror Shot, Acid Armor, Ice Beam, Hail, Mirror Coat, Blizzard, Sheer Cold

Vanillish can control ice particles to surround its opponents and freeze them solid. In hot weather, its icy body is in danger of melting, although this Pokémon can be frozen again to restore it to health.

EVOLUTION

Vanillite → Vanillish → Vanilluxe

VANILLITE

Fresh Snow Pokémon

How to Say It: vuh-NIHL-lyte

Type: Ice

Imperial Height: 1'04"

Metric Height: 0.4 m

Imperial Weight: 12.6 lbs.

Metric Weight: 5.7 kg

Possible Moves: Icicle Spear, Harden, Astonish, Uproar, Icy Wind, Mist, Avalanche, Taunt, Mirror Shot, Acid Armor, Ice Beam, Hail, Mirror Coat, Blizzard, Sheer Cold

EVOLUTION

Vanillite → Vanillish → Vanilluxe

Vanillite is particularly popular in Alola and other warm places, because hugging this icy Pokémon is a lovely way to cool off. It can breathe out tiny crystals of ice to create a snow flurry around itself.

VANILLUXE

Snowstorm Pokémon

How to Say It:
vuh-NIHL-lux

Type: Ice

Imperial Height: 4'03"

Metric Height: 1.3 m

Imperial Weight: 126.8 lbs.

Metric Weight: 57.5 kg

Possible Moves: Freeze-Dry, Weather Ball, Icicle Spear, Harden, Astonish, Uproar, Icy Wind, Mist, Avalanche, Taunt, Mirror Shot, Acid Armor, Ice Beam, Hail, Mirror Coat, Blizzard, Sheer Cold

Vanilluxe has two heads, each with a mind of its own, and they don't always agree. When they decide to work together, this Pokémon can create impressive blizzards with the snow clouds it forms inside its body.

EVOLUTION

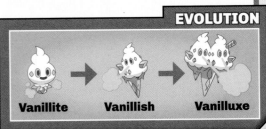

Vanillite → **Vanillish** → **Vanilluxe**

VAPOREON

Bubble Jet Pokémon

How to Say It: vay-POUR-ree-on

Type: Water

Imperial Height: 3'03"

Metric Height: 1.0 m

Imperial Weight: 63.9 lbs.

Metric Weight: 29.0 kg

Possible Moves: Water Gun, Helping Hand, Tackle, Tail Whip, Sand Attack, Baby-Doll Eyes, Quick Attack, Water Pulse, Aurora Beam, Aqua Ring, Acid Armor, Haze, Muddy Water, Last Resort, Hydro Pump

Vaporeon lives near water, and some who see it wandering the shore think it's a mermaid! When submerged, its camouflage is perfect—it can disappear entirely in order to launch a sneak attack.

EVOLUTION

Eevee → **Vaporeon**

VIBRAVA

Vibration Pokémon

How to Say It: VY-BRAH-va

Type: Ground-Dragon

Imperial Height: 3'07"

Metric Height: 1.1 m

Imperial Weight: 33.7 lbs.

Metric Weight: 15.3 kg

Possible Moves: Dragon Breath, Sand Attack, Sonic Boom, Feint Attack, Bide, Mud-Slap, Bulldoze, Sand Tomb, Rock Slide, Supersonic, Screech, Earth Power, Bug Buzz, Earthquake, Sandstorm, Uproar, Hyper Beam, Boomburst

Vibrava has to eat a lot to fuel the growth of its underdeveloped wings. Instead of flying, it vibrates its wings together, creating ultrasonic waves that it uses in battle.

EVOLUTION

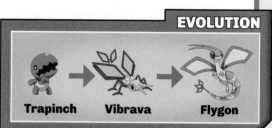

Trapinch → Vibrava → Flygon

VIKAVOLT

Levitate Pokémon

How to Say It: VIE-kuh-volt

Type: Bug-Electric

Imperial Height: 4'11"

Metric Height: 1.5 m

Imperial Weight: 99.2 lbs.

Metric Weight: 45.0 kg

Possible Moves: Thunderbolt, Air Slash, Charge, Vice Grip, String Shot, Mud-Slap, Bite, Bug Bite, Spark, Acrobatics, Guillotine, Bug Buzz, Dig, Zap Cannon, Agility

Vikavolt uses its large jaws to focus the electricity it produces inside its body, then unleashes a powerful zap to stun its opponents. Flying-type Pokémon that once posed a threat are no match for its shocking attacks.

EVOLUTION

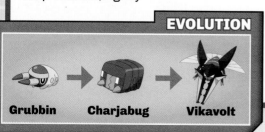

Grubbin → Charjabug → Vikavolt

VULLABY

Diapered Pokémon

How to Say It: VUL-luh-bye

Type: Dark-Flying

Imperial Height: 1'08"

Metric Height: 0.5 m

Imperial Weight: 19.8 lbs.

Metric Weight: 9.0 kg

Possible Moves: Gust, Leer, Fury Attack, Pluck, Nasty Plot, Flatter, Feint Attack, Punishment, Defog, Tailwind, Air Slash, Dark Pulse, Embargo, Whirlwind, Brave Bird, Mirror Move

Vullaby wears bones around its lower half as a shield, and it replaces the bones as it outgrows them. Its wings aren't yet big enough to carry it through the air.

EVOLUTION

Vullaby   Mandibuzz

VULPIX (Alola Form)

Fox Pokémon

How to Say It: VULL-picks

Type: Ice

Imperial Height: 2'00"

Metric Height: 0.6 m

Imperial Weight: 21.8 lbs.

Metric Weight: 9.9 kg

Possible Moves: Powder Snow, Tail Whip, Roar, Baby-Doll Eyes, Ice Shard, Confuse Ray, Icy Wind, Payback, Mist, Feint Attack, Hex, Aurora Beam, Extrasensory, Safeguard, Ice Beam, Imprison, Blizzard, Grudge, Captivate, Sheer Cold

Vulpix in the Alola region was once known as Keokeo, and some older folks still use that name. Its six tails can create a spray of ice crystals to cool itself off when it gets too hot.

EVOLUTION

Vulpix   Ninetales

WAILMER

Ball Whale Pokémon

How to Say It: WAIL-murr

Type: Water

Imperial Height: 6'07"

Metric Height: 2.0 m

Imperial Weight: 286.6 lbs.

Metric Weight: 130.0 kg

Possible Moves: Splash, Growl, Water Gun, Rollout, Whirlpool, Astonish, Water Pulse, Mist, Brine, Rest, Water Spout, Amnesia, Dive, Bounce, Hydro Pump, Heavy Slam

When Wailmer is feeling playful, it inflates its round body by sucking in seawater, then bounces joyfully around. It releases the water in a showy way by shooting impressive spouts from its nostrils.

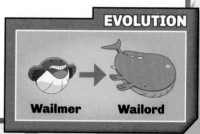

EVOLUTION

Wailmer → Wailord

WAILORD

Float Whale Pokémon

How to Say It: WAIL-ord

Type: Water

Imperial Height: 47'07"

Metric Height: 14.5 m

Imperial Weight: 877.4 lbs.

Metric Weight: 398.0 kg

Possible Moves: Soak, Noble Roar, Heavy Slam, Splash, Growl, Water Gun, Rollout, Whirlpool, Astonish, Water Pulse, Mist, Brine, Rest, Water Spout, Amnesia, Dive, Bounce, Hydro Pump

Wailord swim with their mouths open to gather food. In some places, pods of these enormous Pokémon become a tourist attraction of sorts, as visitors go out in boats to see if they can spot one.

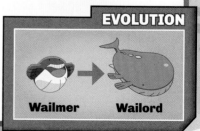

EVOLUTION

Wailmer → Wailord

WEAVILE

Sharp Claw Pokémon

How to Say It: WEE-vile

Type: Dark-Ice

Imperial Height: 3'07"

Metric Height: 1.1 m

Imperial Weight: 75.0 lbs.

Metric Weight: 34.0 kg

Possible Moves: Embargo, Revenge, Assurance, Scratch, Leer, Taunt, Quick Attack, Feint Attack, Icy Wind, Fury Swipes, Nasty Plot, Metal Claw, Hone Claws, Fling, Screech, Night Slash, Snatch, Punishment, Dark Pulse

In the cold places where they live, Weavile communicate with others in their group by carving up rocks and trees with their sharp claws. In the Alola region, they often battle with the cold-dwelling Sandshrew and Vulpix.

EVOLUTION

Sneasel → Weavile

WHIMSICOTT

Windveiled Pokémon

How to Say It: WHIM-sih-kot

Type: Grass-Fairy

Imperial Height: 2'04"

Metric Height: 0.7 m

Imperial Weight: 14.6 lbs.

Metric Weight: 6.6 kg

Possible Moves: Growth, Leech Seed, Mega Drain, Cotton Spore, Gust, Tailwind, Hurricane, Moonblast

Whimsicott is so light and fluffy that it drifts on the wind. The cotton that covers its body is easily shed, whether Whimsicott is making a mess in someone's home or being blown about by a strong wind.

EVOLUTION

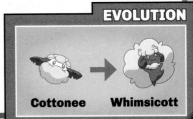

Cottonee → Whimsicott

WHISCASH

Whiskers Pokémon

How to Say It: WISS-cash

Type: Water-Ground

Imperial Height: 2'11"

Metric Height: 0.9 m

Imperial Weight: 52.0 lbs.

Metric Weight: 23.6 kg

Possible Moves: Thrash, Belch, Zen Headbutt, Tickle, Mud-Slap, Mud Sport, Water Sport, Water Gun, Mud Bomb, Amnesia, Water Pulse, Magnitude, Rest, Snore, Aqua Tail, Earthquake, Muddy Water, Future Sight, Fissure

Whiscash lives in the swamp, where it rests on the murky bottom most of the time, waiting for food to float by. If you see one leaping energetically out of the water, it might mean an earthquake is threatening.

EVOLUTION

Barboach → Whiscash

WIGGLYTUFF

Balloon Pokémon

How to Say It: WIG-lee-tuff

Type: Normal-Fairy

Imperial Height: 3'03"

Metric Height: 1.0 m

Imperial Weight: 26.5 lbs.

Metric Weight: 12.0 kg

Possible Moves: Double-Edge, Play Rough, Sing, Defense Curl, Disable, Double Slap

EVOLUTION

Igglybuff → Jigglypuff → Wigglytuff

When the weather gets warm, Wigglytuff shed their fur, which can be spun into delightfully soft yarn. As these Pokémon breathe in, their bodies expand to hold more air—sometimes they make a game of how much they can inflate.

WIMPOD

Turn Tail Pokémon

How to Say It: WIM-pod

Type: Bug-Water

Imperial Height: 1'08"

Metric Height: 0.5 m

Imperial Weight: 26.5 lbs.

Metric Weight: 12.0 kg

Possible Moves: Struggle Bug, Sand Attack

When the cowardly Wimpod flees from battle, it leaves a path swept clean by the passing of its many legs. It helps keep the beaches and seabeds clean, too, scavenging just about anything edible.

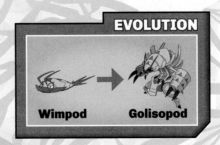

EVOLUTION

Wimpod → Golisopod

WINGULL

Seagull Pokémon

How to Say It: WING-gull

Type: Water-Flying

Imperial Height: 2'00"

Metric Height: 0.6 m

Imperial Weight: 20.9 lbs.

Metric Weight: 9.5 kg

Possible Moves: Growl, Water Gun, Supersonic, Wing Attack, Mist, Water Pulse, Quick Attack, Air Cutter, Pursuit, Aerial Ace, Roost, Agility, Air Slash, Hurricane

Wingull's bones are hollow, allowing it to soar effortlessly. If several Wingull are circling in one spot above the sea, fishermen take note and cast their lines in that area for a good catch.

EVOLUTION

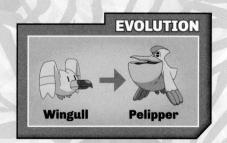

Wingull → Pelipper

WISHIWASHI

Small Fry Pokémon

School Form

Solo Form

How to Say It:
WISH-ee-WASH-ee

Type: Water

Imperial Height: Solo Form: 0'08" / School Form: 26'11"

Metric Height: Solo Form: 0.2 m / School Form: 8.2 m

Imperial Weight: Solo Form: 0.7 lbs. / School Form: 173.3 lbs.

Metric Weight: Solo Form: 0.3 kg / School Form: 78.6 kg

Possible Moves: Water Gun, Growl, Helping Hand, Feint Attack, Brine, Aqua Ring, Tearful Look, Take Down, Dive, Beat Up, Aqua Tail, Double-Edge, Soak, Endeavor, Hydro Pump

If a Wishiwashi looks like it's about to cry, watch out! The light that shines from its watering eyes draws the entire school, and they band together to fight off their opponent by sheer strength of numbers.

EVOLUTION
Does not evolve.

XURKITREE

Glowing Pokémon

Ultra Beast

How to Say It:
ZURK-ih-tree

Type: Electric

Imperial Height: 12'06"

Metric Height: 3.8 m

Imperial Weight: 220.5 lbs.

Metric Weight: 100.0 kg

Possible Moves: Tail Glow, Spark, Charge, Wrap, Thunder Shock, Thunder Wave, Shock Wave, Ingrain, Thunder Punch, Eerie Impulse, Signal Beam, Thunderbolt, Hypnosis, Discharge, Electric Terrain, Power Whip, Ion Deluge, Zap Cannon

Xurkitree, one of the mysterious Ultra Beasts, invaded an electric plant after it emerged from the Ultra Wormhole. Some suspect it absorbs electricity into its body to power the serious shocks it gives off.

EVOLUTION
Does not evolve.

189

YUNGOOS

Loitering Pokémon

How to Say It: YUNG-goose

Type: Normal

Imperial Height: 1'04"

Metric Height: 0.4 m

Imperial Weight: 13.2 lbs.

Metric Weight: 6.0 kg

Possible Moves: Tackle, Leer, Pursuit, Sand Attack, Odor Sleuth, Bide, Bite, Mud-Slap, Super Fang, Take Down, Scary Face, Crunch, Hyper Fang, Yawn, Thrash, Rest

Yungoos is always on the move during the day, looking for food—and it's not too picky about what it bites with its sharp teeth. When night comes, it immediately falls asleep no matter where it happens to be.

EVOLUTION

Yungoos   Gumshoos

ZUBAT

Bat Pokémon

How to Say It: ZOO-bat

Type: Poison-Flying

Imperial Height: 2'07"

Metric Height: 0.8 m

Imperial Weight: 16.5 lbs.

Metric Weight: 7.5 kg

Possible Moves: Absorb, Supersonic, Astonish, Bite, Wing Attack, Confuse Ray, Air Cutter, Swift, Poison Fang, Mean Look, Leech Life, Haze, Venoshock, Air Slash, Quick Guard

Being in the sun isn't healthy for Zubat, so it spends the day sleeping in caves. Since it doesn't have eyes, it uses ultrasonic waves to detect its surroundings.

EVOLUTION

Zubat → Golbat → Crobat

ZYGARDE

Order Pokémon

How to Say It: ZY-gard

Type: Dragon-Ground

Imperial Height: 16'05"

Metric Height: 5.0 m

Imperial Weight: 672.4 lbs.

Metric Weight: 305.0 kg

Legendary Pokémon

Possible Moves: Glare, Bulldoze, Dragon Breath, Bite, Safeguard, Dig, Bind, Land's Wrath, Sandstorm, Haze, Crunch, Earthquake, Camouflage, Dragon Pulse, Coil, Outrage

When Zygarde has gathered 50 percent of its Cells, it takes on this serpentine Forme. It is said that this Legendary Pokémon is a guardian of the ecosystem, and that it could become even more powerful.

EVOLUTION
Does not evolve.